Online Dating: Searching for the
Holy Grail in Cyberspace

Kaeley Glasco

This book is dedicated to all of the romantics, and cynics, searching for love, and a life partner in virtual-reality.

Introduction

Cyberspace is defined as, all of the data stored in a large computer or network represented as a three-dimensional model through which a virtual-reality user can move. Not exactly a romantic notion. Yet online dating is a force, in the coupling of many a new breed relationships and marriages.

The once upon a time storybook fairy tales of handsome knights and beautiful princesses, living happily ever after, seems like childhood fantasies. Little did they know that one day finding your princess, would involve browsing an online catalog of fair damsels, and tapping a key may be the starting point of finding your own personal happily ever after.

So who are these daters, turned couples, turned husbands and wives? What is the secret to their success in using one of the most impersonal forms of communication, to catch lightening in a bottle, in finding a soul mate, marriage partner, the love of their life?

In studying the online dating phenomena, and documenting it via published online articles for over 5-years, in addition to collecting feedback from online daters regaling their successful experiences; I present the top 50+ of my most compelling online dating columns. The advice will help the beginner, and longtime user of online dating sites, to accomplish their goal in successfully finding a life-partner. Other practical advice includes suggestions in enhancing your relationship e.g. what to do after you have met your match, and navigating common couple issues that will arise sooner or later in long-term relationships.

Table of Contents

Weeding out Players and Gold diggers
So exactly how old are your online dating photos?
The thin line between Sexy and Trashy
Red flags and deal breakers
Relocation for love

Single for life or online dating?
Looking for love in all the right places
Travelling to find true love
When to say Y-E-S to S-E-X
Mix it up: Top 5 steps for the fearless girl to find her perfect match
Seduction 101: A man's guide to get her in the mood
Last Call... The bar scene is officially over

Standard or Niche dating sites: Finding the right dating site for you
Sex and Politics - Dating by Political Party
The 800 Pound Gorilla - Big Box Dating Sites

Sugar Daddies and Sugar Babies - Travel for free dating sites
Looks first and ask questions later, those 'Tinder' moments
Mixing business, pleasure and romance - Meetup App
I heart Jesus, how about you?

Women and Men who lie about their age
Are children a deal breaker?
Doe's race really matter?
Sex with no strings attached
Fit or Fat - What is your true body-type?
Height Stereotype - Is taller, better?
Dating and Fitness - When a few extra pounds is a few too many
Age stereotype - Should women hide their age?

Who's paying?
How to deal with negative and toxic people
Dealing with rejection
Exit strategies for dead-end relationships

Valentine's Day

A Singleton's guide to holiday fun
Out of the Box Valentine's Day for Singles
Why Saint Patrick's Day is more fun for
Singles

Breaking the dating slump
Starting over after age 50
Are you a serial dater?

Why Blue Eyes are HOT
The Attachment Theory- Some people suck
and they will die alone
Soulmates and Love at first sight - Fact not
fiction

Tired of being single? Buy a mate
Is bad credit a deal breaker for future couple
purchases?
Dating military personnel and other long-
term business transient

Part One: Online Dating Game Plan

Searching for the Holy Grail

So you think you may want to embark upon Online Dating as an alternative means of finding true love? Well, there are a few things to consider before you upload a couple of out of focus pictures and write a sloppy off the cuff synopsis about why you are the greatest man or woman created since Adam or Eve. And then sit back and wait for the offers to start pouring in.

First things first, you need to understand your own rationale for considering online dating. What are your expectations? You need to be as realistic as possible in what you are searching for in a potential mate. If you have a long list of characteristics that you find appealing in a mate and you are looking to tick-off the list when you meet someone; you are wasting your time and your new interest's time.

Be concise, select four or five of the core qualities you find most appealing and the rest will come into play as you get to know your new love interest over time. There is no logical way to immediately size up a person to determine if he or she has twenty intrinsic or learned qualities. If you are prone to being shallow and judgmental about the people you meet, without making any real effort to get to know them? This may take a while! And you could ultimately lose a golden opportunity.

Example of first date, bad snap judgements; "She didn't seem to respond to my sexy flirting, I think she may be a little uptight or fidget." This gal may very well be a wildcat in the boudoir and a perfectly refined lady in public. "His career choice doesn't really have many high paying jobs, so I don't think he will be a good provider." You may have just allowed the world's greatest dad, and most loving father, to your future children, to slip through your fingers.

It's easy to cling to the age old, trite anecdotes; "If it's meant to be it will be" or "When the right one comes along I'll know." Um, not really. If you continue using shallow tactics to alienate people, you may in reality be alienating a perfectly suitable mate.

The ideology of finding a perfect person or

counterpart who completes you as a human being is highly romanticized. Does this romanticism create unrealistic expectations in our search for a mate? Are we deterring and deferring our happiness by searching for the idea of a person and not a real person? For answers to these and other thought provoking questions, please stand by. Relax, being over 30 or 40, and single is a little cock-eyed, but it's not fatal. The fact of the matter is dating is a process. It's fun and at times tedious, draining process; that is if you're doing it right. There are many online dating sites to choose from.

The big box, highly marketed Match dot com and eHarmony, to niche sites like Christian Singles, Plenty of Fish, etc. Choose an online dating site that is best suited for your personal interest. Perhaps even try two online dating sites, one with a monthly paid access and one with free access. Which one is better? You be the judge.

I recommend getting semiprofessional photos taken for your online dating profile. Unclench your wallet; I'm not talking Annie Leibowitz here. Sears Portrait Studio, it's not just for children's photos anymore. It offers a "Business Package." Not that you need to wear business attire. Feel free to bring one business/casual or business/formal event wear, or all casual, your call. Also one head shot is included. Stay away from wacky photos; it's a thin line between whimsical and silly. Fun and dignified is a good start.

One of the most important tools used to attract the opposite sex is your online dating, written profile. This can appear with or without photos. If you don't post a photo male or female, most viewers will assume you have something to hide or you are not attractive. This may be true.

However, some attractive, intelligent men and women use this non photo technique to "force" the reading of his or her profile. This tactic forces the interested party to read what he or she has to say VS simply seeing an attractive photo and responding based on the photo without a clue of what you are seeking in a man or woman. It's a little risky as you may be overlooked by the very people you want to attract. I recommend photos. If you feel shy or in any way embarrassed about having your pictures on a dating website? Get over it.

When preparing your profile be concise in your writing; one paragraph for each of the following;

1. Talk about your hobbies and interest, new and exciting things you would love to try.

2. Talk about your accomplishments and any interesting future aspirations, everyone love's a winner.

3. Talk about yourself and what you are seeking in a mate, briefly and no list!

4. Your taste in music, movies, favorite food.

This is just the beginning, and you're on your way to a new and exciting phase, with greatly fun possibilities.

Weeding out Players and Gold diggers

Love is the name of the game. Yes, game. If you think it should be natural, spontaneous and just happen; I hate to burst your bubble, but the new reality of dating is, "the upgrade." One of the many games people play in the world of online dating. The upgrade is the baser and shallower aspect of dating in the new millennium. Some men want to date the youngest, hottest and most attractive women that they can attract, and will use many tactics to do so. Some women want the richest, most attractive men that they can attract or lure in. So if you're not Bill Gates or a Supermodel where does that leave you in the pecking order of desirability? Ah, isn't it romantic.

Have you gone out on a date with someone you contacted online and had the distinct feeling that you were being judged, analyzed and basically sized-up? You were probably right in your feelings.

Your companion may have been searching for flaws or reasons to reject you rather than making an earnest effort to get to know you. The process of elimination is just one of the many dating games. When a man of average looks wants to date attractive women who look like Victoria's Secret lingerie models, (yeah, good luck with that!) he may consciously or unconsciously seek reasons to eliminate women of average looks or an average body by nitpicking. Men aren't the only ones guilty of this.

Hey guys have you ever went to a gal's home to pick her up for a date and she takes one look at your car and pauses? She looks at your clothes and shoes with a subtle or not so subtle hint of disapproval? She cross examines you about your career choice and the related finances? Well, you're being sized-up too. She may go through with the date and make the best of it or she may find an excuse to cut it short, but make no mistake, there is a possibility that you have been eliminated from any future dates with the gold digger types.

If you're wondering can people be this shallow and materialistic? The answer is yes! Naturally people have preferences in what they find appealing in the opposite sex. But try to be realistic, sincere and most of all fair. Not just to the other person, but to yourself. It's great to have high standards, but being too rigid is a good recipe for disappointment.

So where does "love" fit into the scheme of things? It seems so removed. Meanwhile after your first or second date, you're waiting to find out if you qualified to proceed to the next round! How does one discern the shallow nitpickers and materialistic gold diggers from the sincere people, looking for something real? Being alert to the games helps. But communication is the key. There are usually some hints in the online profile as to the person's nature or agenda. Before meeting, I like to ask the question; where do you see yourself in 3 years?

Yes, it sounds like an interview question, but goals can, and should be set on multiple levels, career and personal. If his answer is silly or evasive? This could be a red flag. If she drones on reciting a vast list of material things that she wants? It could be a hint. I am in no way advocating snap judgements; I'm just saying take all of it into consideration.

A good rule of thumb is to date a cross section of men or women with varying looks and backgrounds. If you normally date blonds? Date a brunette. Or vice versa. Latin, Asian, Multiracial, mix it up. The same advice to the ladies, mix it up girls! As for money, financial security is great, I highly recommend it. Money offers some assurances in life. There are far more qualities to be considered and appreciated. Basically, decent folks need to stick together and let the shallow types have at it. Because in the end a relationship built on a foundation of shallowness, materialism and aesthetics is bound to crash and burn anyway. Perhaps a link to the fifty percent divorce rate in the USA? Choosing the wrong people for the wrong reasons is a no win situation.

So exactly how old are your online dating photos?

"Time and tide wait for no man" or woman. The aging process is inevitable. While some people choose to accept it, and age graciously, others fight it, deny it, and flat out lie about it! Good genes, Botox, liposuction, cosmetic surgery and other procedures my stave off the natural course of aging. If you're lucky, you will buy a few more precious years of a slightly more youthful appearance. But rest assured the irreversible signs of aging are in the mail. Some men and women seem to be defying the changes.

One of the most awesome things about online dating is the inclusion factor. Men and Women of all ages, all stages, all walks of life and all levels of attractiveness are WELCOME! The oldest man with a profile on a very popular dating website is age 83. I've searched dating websites in other major cities and found hopeful daters at age 94. How absolutely marvelous! Love is eternal.

One of the major pet peeves in the online dating chat rooms and blog postings; is the topic of outdated profile photos. There are people who post photos from upwards of 20 years ago. I've even seen profiles with postings of the user's childhood photos? Why? What are they thinking? Perhaps it's a sentimental yearning for the simpler days of the past? Or maybe they think that their baby pictures are really, really cute. Either way the answer is no. Fast forward to the present. Profile pictures should be as current as possible, date stamped or noted as to how long ago it was taken. Try to update your profile photos every 4-6 months, depending on how long you remain on a particular dating site.

You may have been a lot sexier when you were much younger or even 10 years ago; posting outdated pictures to your profile page in which you look totally different now, is completely deceptive. If your self-esteem is somehow linked to the glory days of your youth? Feel free to post "then and now" pictures, that's pretty cool as long as you remember to include a current "now" photo.

The thin line between Sexy and Trashy

Imagine a good looking shirtless hottie with perfect 6-pack abs; he's flexing and posing in a bathroom mirror and takes an impromptu picture of him to post on his dating web page. Or perhaps a scantily clad woman posing in her skimpiest thong bikini, showing as much skin as humanly possible, and posting the picture on her dating web page. These sorts of pictures can be found on every online dating site in any city.

Exactly what are the intentions and motivation in posting these specific types of sexy photos? Is it self-promotion or self-exploitation? Perhaps a bit of both. Are they simply proud of their bodies and have worked very hard to develop that golden physique, and want to flaunt their efforts?

Maybe? Or they just really want attention, recognition and admiration based on their looks. Does this mean that they're shallow? Not necessarily. However, if you are the type of person who is interested and lured in by these images based on their looks? Perhaps you're the one who is shallow.

Attractive people tend to have liberties extended to them freely, based on their appeal. Are you are willing to sign-on as one of their many admirers? Okay, take a number and get in line! It's not their fault if people choose to flatter, cater to, and chase after them because they're attractive.

Fair warning to all of those "Players" who are using their good looks to get by; you better have something more to offer other than good looks or you may find yourself reduced to "Cougar" bait, in the online dating arena. It's the unfortunate backlash for sending out the wrong message to the wrong people.

Instead of being worshipped, you may end up being exploited, ridiculed or labelled as an attractive airhead. I am all for individual expression through fashion, but there's a thin line between sexy and trashy. Make no mistake, in no way do you have to live your life or make choices based on other people's random opinions of you.

On the other hand, being tastefully dressed is always in style and a great choice. Besides, true sex appeal comes from within it's akin to an internal self-confidence. You either have it or you don't. Faking sex appeal by wearing skimpy outfits, or exposing yourself, may backfire. Sure, you're great looking eye candy to ogle, but will anyone take you seriously?

In the online dating game, the first impression sets a tone, like it or not. Your pictures and what's written in your profile lead people to make assumptions about you, based on the viewer's interpretation of what they are seeing and reading.

Red flags and deal breakers

Online dating is fun and exciting. The possibilities are endless. There's always someone new joining the ranks of hopeful daters. Depending on which city you reside in the possibilities can be overwhelming.

So how does one weed-out the frogs to find a prince or princess? Sometimes we have difficulties pinpointing our exact perfect match. Yes, there is always the list of obligatory traits and characteristics used as a guideline to determine whom we are seeking; but when faced with great deal of sexual attraction and chemistry, sometimes that list tends to fly out of the window. Whether your potential love interest is relatively attractive or drop dead gorgeous, certain behavior should be treated as unacceptable and definitely a deal breaker.

We all like to blow off a little steam, unwind and let our hair down, so to speak. A cocktail or two at an after work gathering is just the ticket. However, when a cocktail or two turns into 6-10? Red flag! Head for the hills. There is no celebration or disappointment that warrants the excessive consumption of alcohol. Heavy drinking implies alcoholism or a reckless lack of self-control. In either case, deal breaker.

The decisions made by two consenting adults related to sex, on any terms, is subject to personal preferences. However, if your date is too sexually aggressive in an inappropriate period of time in relation to meeting, this may be a red flag warning that your date is interested in a sexual conquest VS anything more serious. Depending on the personality, some people like to appear impressive in an attempt to impress others. Major red flag alert if your potential love interest lies to you to impress, or mislead you. This may include embellished details about their employment, education, or interest. Prior to meeting, it could include inaccuracies about height, weight, relationship status, etc.

If it sounds too good to be true, it may not be true. Although I do believe that most people are truthful, we all need to read the signals and steer clear of those individuals whose intentions or habits don't match our needs. Remember to be selective when choosing dates. This may lead to fewer dates but in the long run, choosing quality over quantity will make for better dating experiences.

Relocation for love

Despite the recession woes, the U.S. still has a lot to offer in terms of quality of life and opportunities. Albeit some areas of the country are experiencing high unemployment and foreclosures; there are other areas of the nation where the unemployment rate is well below the national average and the foreclosure rate is low. Sometimes the grass really is greener on the other side.

In the Forbes dot com survey for "Best Cities for Singles" it examined U.S. metropolitan statistical areas in seven different categories: coolness, cost of living alone, culture, job growth, online dating participation, nightlife and the ratio of singles to the entire population of the metro. The best cities for singles are as follows:

1. New York City

2. Boston

3. Chicago

4. Seattle

5. Washington DC

6. Atlanta

7. San Francisco

8. Los Angeles

9. Milwaukee

10. Philadelphia

If you are fortunate enough to work for a national company with multiple locations throughout the US, you may want to consider transferring to a city that has more to offer! It may seem like a big decision to relocate, but think of it as a big adventure and an opportunity for a fresh start. Who knows? You may just fall in love with your new home and wonder why you didn't go for it sooner. It's a big world out there with more opportunities than you imagine.

Part Two: Why Love Now?

Single for life or online dating?

If you're single and relatively attractive with a nice personality and clever writing skills; you will be vehemently sought after and highly desired in the online dating arena. Wait a minute, if you're so great; how come you're still single? I'll tell you why. The traditional ways in which singles meet are dwindling and becoming less and less desirable for reasons that are beyond our control. Although still a means, trying to meet a future mate in any one of the following scenarios may produce less than desirable results;

Work: Fishing off the company pier is generally frowned upon in the wake of sexual harassment lawsuits and anti-fraternizing policies between employees in the work place. Other drawbacks are, being the subject of petty office gossip and the risk of appearing unprofessional in your dealings with colleagues. Not to mention the awkwardness in facing your ex-lover five days a week after the fling is flung.

Back to School for the MBA: Kudos! Continuing your education after years of being far removed from the practices associated with the matriculation process e.g. studying etc., may require additional focus and effort. If coupled with working full time and having a somewhat dynamic work load, dating someone in the same busy boat, may create scheduling challenges. You're better off with someone who does not have as many "balls in the air." A partner with a lighter schedule may be more flexible to work around your busy schedule. Besides an online MBA program may be an alternate solution offering even more flexibility. Unless of course, you simply prefer the class room experience? Aren't you a little bit too old to play beer pong and quarters?

Matchmaking by friends and family: Just say no! Unless your friends or family really knows what turns you on? They are just trying to set you up using a "cookie cutter" notion of what they think you will like. Albeit their intentions are good, ones' own personal romantic life is better left in ones' own hands. You don't want to end up kicking yourself for allowing someone else to foist you into an awkward blind date. Whereas you are so grossly mismatched that you are wondering if your companion is even from the same planet. If you value your time as I do, you will want to make more suitable choices on how you spend your evenings.

Bars/Night Clubs: I'll admit it's a classic! But, not at all conducive to holding meaningful conversations and getting to know a person on a real level. Bars and the over indulgence of alcohol go hand in hand. Not the best state of mind for making "sober" decisions. Although fun and certainly entertaining, encounters that occur in this venue are best taken as a night's fun experience and not necessarily offering a future endeavor.

Fitness Centers: I don't know about you, but I don't think sweat drenched hair is a good look! When a woman goes to the gym in full make-up and sexy spandex and is more interested in preening than working out; men tend to notice her, but not in a good way. She looks obvious, on the prowl and maybe even a tad bit desperate. So ladies, what's your choice? Desperation or perspiration? When you go to the gym, go there to take care of your body. If a chance meeting occurs, terrific. Besides any guy who approaches you when you're all sweaty, out of breath and without make-up, probably has a genuine interest.

On the flip side, the initial encounter via Online, a meeting or a date, has fewer pitfalls. The coffee house meeting. Could anything be more trite and boring! It's a good thing that coffee is available to stave off the urge to nap! In case you haven't guessed by now, I am not a proponent of coffee houses as an ideal location for meeting singles and it's certainly not a date. The coffee house meeting is probably the most popular meeting suggestion, by men, for a first meeting. Why? It's the cheapest way for a man to meet as many women as possible without spending money. Basically, it's a cheap non-date.

Guys, I'm not saying break the bank, but if you are playing a numbers game and indiscriminately soliciting a large number of women without any personal consideration for the gals as individuals? You are wasting the gal's time. I suggest you focus on a smaller number of women and get to know them a little better before meeting. If there is any sincere interest or a spark, then you can make a proper date plan. I know it's the company more so than the location, regarding the coffee shop. But get real, who wants to drive 15-20 miles, one way, for a cup coffee? Ladies be fair too. Suffice to say you can date 10 men and it won't cost us one red cent. Men bear the brunt of the cost related to dating, in general. Try to find a happy medium.

Looking for love in all the right places

If you've decided that the time is right to pursue a long term relationship, great! But as a busy professional, are you prepared to actively pursue dating as a time consuming process? A whirlwind romance seems like a very romantic notion. Being swept away by an overpowering and compelling infatuation, followed by a quick nuptial after a few weeks, and you're hitched! It happens. But the practicality of this action is debatable by some. Since when is love practical?

For you more conservative types who spend half of your life rationalizing your long list of demands and expectations in a future spouse, it could be a long ride. Or if an active social life is an after-thought in your scheme of things, you may want to take a moment to prioritize the value of finding a life-partner.

Make an effort to gain a balance between your work life, obligations, and your social life. You'll be glad you did. A happy, active social life adds to your quality of life. Research shows that there are psychological and physical health benefits associated with being in a stable and loving long term relationship e.g. marriage.

Married people enjoy longer lives. Studies show the difference in death rates between single and married people starts in the 40s and continues across the lifespan. The difference spikes in the 70-84 year old age group where the death rate for single people is almost double that of their married counterparts.

According to the Health and Human Services report, getting married and staying married reduces depression in both men and women. Social isolation is linked to higher rates of depression. Marriage also contributes to a decline in heavy drinking and drug abuse especially among young adults.

Research is just beginning to reveal how strong this link can be. A study in the Journal of Family Psychology shows happiness in one's life depends more on the quality of family relationships than on the level of income. There is scientific evidence that shows the power of love trumps the power of money. A happier life is just one of love's greatest benefits, so open your heart and mind to love, and it'll find you.

Traveling to find true love

Love. Is there any feeling more splendid?
Joy, passion, longing, and breathlessness are
some of the feelings associated with sharing
love. Finding your soulmate and sharing true
love can be life changing. How far are you
willing to go to find love? Online dating
sites offer search options that extend from
your city or state, to the entire USA, and
worldwide.

So once again, how far are you willing to go
to find true love? Would you consider dating
someone who lives in another state, beyond
a neighboring state? Would you consider
relocating to a major city to meet more
singles? Would you quit your job, pack up
and move 5,000 miles away from your
home, friends and family to be with your
lover? Or do you want love as long as it's
convenient?

The world is full of many places and many
people. Is it realistic to believe that the one
perfect person for us on the planet lives two
blocks away?

According to dirvorcerate dot org and based
on two separate comprehensive studies; the
divorce rates in the USA are as follows: 1st

marriage 50%, 2nd marriage 67%, 3rd marriage 74%, this data is published by the Forest Institute of Professional Psychology.

In another study published by The Enrichment Journal, it's finding are as follows; 1st marriage 47%, 2nd marriage 60%, 3rd marriage 74%. It appears that when it comes to marriage, the third time is not a charm.

It would also appear that many people are settling for relationships and marriages that are failing on a massive scale. Perhaps a more extensive search for love would be a better path VS spending years of your life in dead end relationships and marriages.

If your job requires extensive travel, or you live in a popular tourist states like Hawaii, Florida, New York. Nevada e.g. Las Vegas etc. You have much greater opportunities of meeting a potential love interest from anywhere around the globe.

If you live in a tourist area, you can set-up your dating profile and leave it open to meeting men or women from any location. That is if you are willing to travel or relocate to continue a love relationship.

When travelling, check out the local singles that have profiles posted on your same online dating site and try to connect with them 2-weeks prior to your travel. Try to connect with the singles that are open to meeting someone from any location, they will be more receptive. With all of this being said, the question still remains; how far are you willing to go to find true love? Expand your options when searching for a soul mate and let nature and destiny take its course.

When to say Y-E-S to S-E-X

You have just met the possible guy or gal of your dreams. This person is funny, smart, likes the same things as you, and is the biggest sweetheart ever. You find yourself incredibly sexually attracted to this person and things start to heat-up quickly. Your heart and your body say giddy up! What's next?

Hopefully your self-control will prevail and you will think about taking a closer look before you leap. For some women, a man who comes on too strong sexually can be a major turn-off. The same situation could apply for the sexually assertive woman, who comes on too strong. If you really like the person, you don't want to blow it. Double entendre aside.

Is physical attraction a huge factor in a relationship, or is it superficial? I'll give you a hint. It can be both. Physical attraction and great sex does not guarantee a long-term relationship. But marginal attraction and lackluster sex can be a deal breaker in some cases, and erode intimacy over time. Here's where having a solid foundation of the following relationship fundamentals will come in handy.

1. Intellectual and Emotional Compatibility (these are two very different things and you need both in harmony)
2. Mutual Interest (things you genuinely enjoy doing together)
3. Respect
4. Empathy

These qualities are some of the prerequisites of love. Throw in the hot and heavy chemistry, and life is good! Can these qualities be determined in another person by a few email messages, several phone calls and one date? Absolutely not.

Avoid being swept away by sexual chemistry resulting in missteps in establishing the appropriate pace and progression, in functional relationship building. It may be a good idea to consider dating protocols. I don't necessarily subscribe to a one-size-fits-all approach to dating, but whether you are 18 or 85 some of the same dating questions apply.

1. When is the right time for the first kiss?
2. Is it too early for a steamy make-out session?
3. When is the time right for sex?

Note: These questions imply that both parties are looking for something more than a sexual fling.

According to a study by Mary Claire Morr-Serewicz of the Department of Human Communication Studies at the University of Denver, and Paul Mongeau of Arizona State University. First dates "represent an important early event in the development of a dating relationship.'

Mongeau's research shows that the term "date" can be condensed into four subcategories:

1. Dyadic: The purpose to which the date is occurring between two individuals.

2. Date cycle: Includes the major behavior components of a date.

3. Positive interaction expectancies: Implies that dates allow each other a chance to get to know one another in a comfortable environment.

4. Sexual overtones: Refers to the part of the date where romantic relationships may develop and/or include sexual attraction or expectation.

These components are the basis of a date, making up its structure and providing a starting place from which to begin the dating process.

Reasons to Date:

In Mongeau's study, he quotes what identifies the seven purposes for dating:

1. Recreation (to have fun)

2. Socialization (to get to know the partner)

3. Status grading (increasing social status by dating an attractive partner)

4. Companionship (finding a friend to do things with)

5. Mate selection/courtship (finding a spouse)

6. Intimacy (establishing a meaningful relationship)

7. Produce a number of relationship outcomes. (e.g., sexual partner, friendship, short-term romantic relationship, or life partnership.)

According to Mongeau's research, these are the primary reasons for going on dates:

1. Recreation
2. Socialization and
3. Companionship

The rest pertains to steps that occur later on in the dating process or in a relationship. 'Getting to know someone, having fun, and becoming friends with a particular person is half of the reason why people date. The other emotional, romantic e.g. sexual half is not usually the main focus during a first date.'

Although sexual chemistry does add an exciting allure to a date, the bottom line is to have a good time on your dates, and it will lead to whatever the both of you decide. Just be sure of what you want and what's comfortable for you, and the rest will develop naturally. It's dating, it's not breaking rocks, so have fun, and wait for the appropriate relationship development to take your relationship to a sexual level.

Mix it up: Top 5 steps for the fearless girl to find her perfect match offline

Finding your perfect match can be a challenge. When searching for Mr. Right, sometimes you may end up with Mr. Right Now, and settling for a relationship that's going nowhere. Or even worse, dating man after man in a seemingly endless cycle with no match, or end in sight. Is there a way to skip some of the wrong relationship drama and find your perfect match?

Here are some steps to get in line with the actions needed to find the perfect man for you.

Step 1. If you see a guy you like, let him know

Step 2. Make sure you are looking in the right places

Step 3. Have the right mindset for meeting men

Step 4. Have fun on your dates

Step 5. Stop playing coy dating games and lead with your heart

Check out the tips on how to achieve these steps.

Step 1. If you see a man you like, let him know

If you see a guy that you think you would like to get to know, approach him, and give him a compliment.

"I like your jacket/shirt/eyewear; it makes you look very sophisticated.
"You have amazing hair, I love long hair/or clean cut, stylish hair' it really suits you." "I noticed you across the room, you are very attractive. I just want to stop to say hello."

Give the compliment sincerely, smile, and go back to what you were doing. If he is interested, he will approach you.

Step 2. Make sure you are looking in the right places

Pro sporting events are jammed packed with men. Go it alone, or go with a friend, have a drink, enjoy a day out. The right guy will notice you no matter how interesting he finds the game.

Other things to consider:

What sort of men do you really like?

Where would this sort of man hang out?

What sort of places do you normally go to meet men?

If you like the sporty type, fit men, don't expect to find them in your local pub at midnight. Try the gym or the local health food store.

Step 3. Have the right mindset for meeting men

Approaching men is cool, just be classy and confident. Some women may be concerned about coming across as pushy, too eager or desperate if they make the first move. Forget about it. If you are confident and outgoing, own it.

When you approach a man, you're not chasing him. All you are doing is letting him know that you would like for him to chase you.

Step 4. Have fun on your dates

Turn negatives into positives, whenever you ask him a question, make sure you 'connect on the answer' before moving on to the next question. The easiest way to do it is to give positive feedback to his answers.

"How was your day Paul?"

Great! Thanks Sarah, I had to give an important presentation at work, and it went really well.

Respond with: "Congratulations! It's such a great feeling when you're well prepared and your effort pays off with a successful outcome."

If he says he had a bad day, his presentation didn't go well. Respond again with positive feedback.

Respond with: "These things happen sometimes in business, there may not have been a solid connection with this particular group. I'm sure that you are normally very successful with your presentations, and your success will continue."

Step 5. Stop playing coy dating games and lead with your heart

Be yourself and don't play games to impress a man. Your perfect match will like you and love you for who you are. He won't have a chance to do this if you don't show your true personality. Dress tastefully if that's your style, do your hair and make-up and keep yourself looking and feeling attractive. Be genuine about your feelings and let a romantic relationship develop naturally by starting with a friendship.

Seduction 101: A man's guide to get her in the mood

Relationships at any stage require some sort of effort. How you approach this fact can affect the quality of communication and intimacy in your relationship.

Look at the needed effort as a labor of love, and you will find ways to keep your relationship fresh and exciting.

Reaching a comfort zone point in a relationship can be satisfying, but it could also create a lull in the sex and romance department.

A once very active love-life can wind-down to a near halt. Here are a few ways to rekindle the spark in your relationship and heat-up an otherwise chilled sex-life. Try one or all of these fires starters to move your couple time in a romantic direction.

1. Side-by-side couples massage, with scented oil, candles and soft lights to help you both drift away from all thoughts of the day.

2. Make-out like teenagers, hold hands, PDAs, take in a romantic movie, and sit in

the back row and neck.

3. Run her a warm bubble bath and then join her. Great for intimacy and a prelude to a hot night of passion.

4. Gently shampoo her hair with a scented conditioning shampoo; it's very sensuous and giving.

5 Get a change of bedroom scenery, by having a one-night-stand with your partner at a swanky hotel.

Last Call... The bar scene is officially over

Bars, night clubs, lounges, restaurant bars and basically any place that houses a wayward collection of misfits congregating, pontificating and boring others to tears with inane chatter, should be avoided as much as possible in favor better options.

I am convinced that "upscale" sports bars, not to be confused with dive sports bars, also amusement theme bars, are the last bastion of hope in an otherwise bleak and pointless night-out, devoid of any real entertainment value.

Whether it's loud and awful music, drunken loudmouths (male or female) or just a random collection of alcoholics getting their nightly fix, the bar scene has lost its luster.

Bars are the absolute worse place for women to go no matter what your reasons or intentions. Sometimes the best intentions can backfire in a bar environment!

A woman can't simply go to a bar these days to have a drinks and relax, without some old creepy guy bending her ear, when she clearly has no interest in him.

The flip side of the coin is the young guys who are totally hammered after drinking a dozen beers. Trying to have a meaningful conversation with these types is a total waste of time.

Besides, an alcohol fueled conversation is going nowhere but downhill, sooner or later. Naturally if you ignore these people you are perceived as anti-social. So what's the point of going there? If your intention is to go to a bar to meet people? Don't waste your time or energy.

Bars are too noisy. To succeed in connecting with someone, inane small talk is not enough. You want to establish a real connection with them. It's hard to do so in a noisy environment, when you have to talk louder than the room's noise level, broadcasting your conversation for rubberneckers to join-in.

Some women don't go to bars to meet men. Contrary to what some men assume. Women go to bars to have fun with their friends or solo to relax, have cocktails and reflect. Some women don't mind talking to fun, attractive men, but they rarely want anything else to happen beyond that.

Bars have negative associations. Drunkenness, debauchery, and hooking up with strange women or men. Women sometimes associate bars with players, and other undesirable men. Another problem with bars is, drinking too much alcohol, and socializing, don't mix. A few drinks, is fine, but once you cross the line with excessive consumption of alcohol, ugly things can happen. You may accost the person in the wrong way. You could do and say dumb things. Not to mention the nasty bar fights, inside, or outside of bars.

If find yourself randomly, or worse regularly, dropping in to bars? You may want to consider if there is a void that you are trying to fill, and find a much better way to use your time.

A great alternative to a dismal bar is a first time viewing of the interesting movie that you missed in the theater. It's an easy as ordering it via pay-per-view. Or perhaps a trip to the movies to check out the latest blockbuster action flick or comedy. Pretty much anything is better than sitting around getting sloshed at a bar.

Amusement theme bars with gaming, offer cocktails, fun activities and are a fun alternative to sitting around slamming back drinks. The airplane flight simulator game and the fast and furious driving games are awesome.

An upscale sports bar will cater to a very different clientele, than your basic dive sports bar. A more sophisticated drinking establish airing a major sporting event is the best time to check-in, if you still want to go the bar route in meeting a mate.

Part Three: Finding the Right Dating Sites and Apps-Reviews

Standard or Niche dating sites: Finding the right dating site for you

The mega popular dating sites boast about the millions of subscribers and success stories associated with the site. What they don't talk about is the number vacant dating profiles and non-paying members, with active dating profiles, and no access to any received email messages.

The most current statistics reflect online dating generates over 1.2 billion dollars per year. There are 54,250,000 single people in the U.S. Match dot com claims to have 21,575,000 members, and e-Harmony claims to have 15,500.000 members.

The average online dater spends $239.00 per year on dating sites. This extends upward of $600.00 per year depending on the specific website and upgraded features. Not only is online dating an investment of your money, it's greatly an investment of your time and energy.

Smaller, niche dating sites may offer better

matching venues based on your interest and what's most important to you in finding a mate. Smaller niche sites may also have email filtering systems that save you a good deal of time by aiding in the sorting process of filtering out email messages from inappropriate interest, from non-compatible users.

Example: If you are a 21-year-old woman is seeking men age 21-30, the dating site's email filter will discard messages from men over age-30. The dating website Plenty of Fish has an automatic age gap cutoff of 14-years, no matter what age range you state as your preference, the system will not deliver email messages from senders who are more than 14-years older than the intended recipient. This feature is great for young women who don't choose to date men who are as old as their dads. Male users have the same rule to thwart the interest of older women.

Very attractive women receive an overwhelming onslaught of email messages in the online dating arena, as do very attractive men. Unfortunately, some of the messages may contain overt sexual comments or inappropriate request. OKCupid dot com had to strengthen its email filters to combat the level of sexually explicit email messages sent to female members. Some of the email messages were so perverse and offensive it caused many Asian female subscribers to abandon the site.

The dating site Her Way dot com, does not allow the men on the site to contact the women on the site. Only the female users have a contact function. Great website for busy and/or picky women who don't want to deal with tons of email messages from unsuitable, random men. There are dating websites which cater to Christians, interracial dating, farmers, fitness buffs, and a wide range hobbies and interests, including your political party lines. So before you depart with your hard earned cash on the mega dating sites, check out a free niche site or two. You may accomplish the same goal without the cash, and extraneous number of hours poring over countless unsuitable dating profiles on the mega sites.

Sex and Politics- Dating by Political Party

Finding the right partner who is compatible on many levels is like finding a rare gem. At times it seems like we find reasons to eliminate people, for valid reasons or for shallow reasons. A staunch republican conservative who is true to his or her beliefs, may have strife in communicating those core beliefs to a person who affiliates with democrat or liberal agendas. Is one's political persuasion the "new" deal breaker?

It certainly can be for some. Political lines run deep, and for those who can't intelligently glean the importance of the topic, they may be viewed as non-savvy, and with wavering sensibilities. There are two new online dating websites which cater to Democrats or Republican daters. The dating sites launched in Oct. 2012, and both sites are rapidly experiencing rapid growth and interest.

Finding your match can be a bit of a task, as is online dating at times, but still, matching up politically is a priority for many people. RedStateDate dot com and BlueStateDate dot com are two dating sites aimed at: "Connecting like-minded people with their running mates."

Alex Fondrier creator and Chief Executive Officer of Political Matchmakers, the company that owns the websites says "it's about finding someone with your shared values. When it comes to long term relationships, when it comes to marriage, when it comes to raising children is when those shared political values become more important."

Political persuasion can be a bone of contention, especially if you are prone to fault finding in a Presidential administration that you did not subscribe to. This can cause strife and put your partner on the defensive.

Being considerate, tactful and mindful of your partner's political sensibilities on either side will help to avoid disagreements related to politics. Remember, the overall consensus of Americans through their voting rights, collectively make the decision to elect all public officials. Your mate need not bear the brunt of your dissatisfaction in that collective decision.

The 800 Pound Gorilla - Big Box Dating Sites

The cost of online dating can add up over time. The monthly or yearly fees vary from site to site ranging up to and over $600.00 per year. In some cases you do get what you pay for, that is some pretty cool personality matching features and reach, which equals a larger selection of singles. Detailing the perks of the Big Box dating sites will quantify the cost.

1. Membership base: Choosing a site with a large, established membership base simply equates to more options. In the narrowing-down process of personal choices, whether you are looking for a mate and considering a certain, height, weight, education level, background, hobbies, and unique interest to match your interest. Smaller sites may not have much of a selection when all personal preferences are considered.

2. Dating site price: Price may be a deal-breaker for someone on a strict budget or fixed income. If you are new to online dating you may not perceive the cost in relation to the value. Larger sites can afford to offer a short, free trial membership, prior to committing.

3. Search options and algorithms: Compatibility matching services offered by top dating sites have successfully suggested thousands of long-term matches based on personality, scientific dimensions of compatibility and other specific qualities.

4. Niche dating categories: Niche categories consider additional matching factors that may or may not be important depending on the individual. Religious, political, marital status e.g. single/never married or divorced, single parent etc.

5. Privacy and security: These features protect your personal information and identity when communicating with others online.

6. Communication features; this area covers the ways in which you can contact a person of interest, email, instant messaging, chat room, or system prepared flirt options.

7. Customer Support: Technical support, customer service by email and by phone, and billing assistance are some of the features that sites offer.

8. Special dating site features: Personality assessments, mobile access to your account are some of the features offered. Some sites offer "real world" mixer events, and group travel opportunities.

9. Online dating news and advice: Some sites offer trends in dating, success stories, safety reminders, and dating advice on how to navigate the world of online dating.

Dating sites like Zoosk, Match.com, Elite Singles, Our Time and eHarmony, are drawing in the most romantic hopefuls. Sugar Daddies and Sugar Babies - Travel for FREE dating sites

Miss Travel dot com is a website geared to matching wealthy men deemed as "generous" who are willing to pay for airfare or use frequent-flyer miles to fly single attractive women to select locations for dating.

The site has been online for one year and promises that the women involved are not professional escorts, but fun loving females who enjoy travelling especially when it's offered for free! The site has two categories, one for men and one for women. "Attractive Traveler" describes the female members and

"Generous Traveler" for the male members.

Female member use the website for free, male members can browse for free and pay if they see a profile of interest. The site boast having thousands of members worldwide. Men can pay and contact the women via email or extend a "travel invitation," directly inviting the woman to travel with him.

Travel options include traveling with men as in accompanying them for travel. Or traveling to the man's home state or country to meet him. All of the travel arrangements are booked through the site.

The site warns its members, "Note: Remember, online dating is risky, and we always recommend that our members practice a common sense approach when meeting a stranger online." The site also offers travel tips to the members and asks that a potential member read the safety tips before joining the site.

The site's top 10 travel destinations include:

1. Las Vegas, United States
2. Bali, Indonesia
3. London, United Kingdom
4. Miami, United States
5. Cancun, Mexico
6. New York, New York
7. Paris, France
8. Dubai, UAE
9. Los Angeles, CA
10. San Francisco, CA

Looks first and ask questions later, those 'Tinder' moments

The buzz continues surrounding the online dating app "Tinder." The app program operates on the basis of offering very little information about the person of interest and relying strictly on looks to select a potential date. The user clicks yes or no on a series of posted photos indicating further interest in the selected user.

The mobile app pretty much bypasses the written profile aspect, which is arguably a key indicator, and the only real clue to glean a sense of what type of person you are considering.

According to the report, the app's creators feel that the key attraction to the app program may be the lack of rejection, because users never know if they've been passed over. Tinder's creators also claim that they've already had 100 million matches since the app launched.

Although the creators claim that the app offers a lack of rejection, what happens when select users don't receive any messages of interest? There is no such thing as a lack of rejection in dating online.

If a user is very attractive he or she could receive scores of responses from grossly incompatible users. Is this an ego boost? Or an enormous waste of time in weeding out shallow, hapless gawkers?

If a person has average looks they can be dismissed in seconds. Attraction takes on many layers outside of looks. Sense of humor, kindness, good family values, respectfulness, to name a few.

The premise of the app reminds one of the note passing in elementary school. Do you like Billy Jones? Check the box "yes" or "no."

Tinder may be the latest fad, but it certainly is not geared for appropriate consideration in choosing a mate or success in dating. In trying this app you should ask yourself; do I want to meet someone right for me, or spend a lot of time inflating the ego of attractive strangers by rating their photos?

Mixing business, pleasure and romance-Meetup App

If you have grown a little bored with the usual online dating sites, perhaps it's time for a new approach to break the monotony. Meetup dot com offers a large variety of activity options for all interests' levels, including meeting singles.

If you are interested in group events such as dining, movies, happy hour socials or just hanging out and watching your favorite TV program with other die-hard fans, there is a group for you.

Meetup has groups throughout the U.S. and abroad. Sample groups include: salsa dancing, cooking, vegan, girl's night out, single dads, etc.

You can start your own group depending on your personal interests, whether it is social or business. If you are interested in fitness, gaming, marketing, pets, ethnic food, wine, business networking, sports, or any topic under the sun; there is an online community of like-minded individuals in your area, arranging events to pursue those interests.

Of course there are many groups for single mixers. Most of the groups are free to join. You would only pay for your own meal, coffee or cocktails at the Meetup location, depending on the venue.

To see the variety of groups in your home or travel areas, go to Meetup dot com, and enter your zip code. The Meetup website is a lifesaver for meeting new friends and acquaintances, especially if you are moving to a new town and you want to meet genuinely friendly locals with similar interest.

Getting started is easy, create your free profile, peruse the group options and events, RSVP to an event of interest and you are all set. On the event date, you show-up at the location and the group host and other members will be there to greet you.

Everyone introduces themselves; there may be icebreaker games, name tags, and lots of chatting. Cocktails help, in moderation of course. I used this app as a trial and it is a great way to network and meet people, without any pressure. The groups are mixed, male and female, so you can find hang out buddies, and business contacts as well as romantic interest.

I heart Jesus, how about you? Christian dating sites

Online dating sites come in a variety of themes. It seems that more and more niche dating sites are surfacing, in an effort to attract new users.

For the sake of this review, the focus is on Christian dating sites. What is your first thought when you think of Christian dating?

Is it an assumption that you must be a bible-thumping, weekly church going, religious zealot, to join? Not so. If you consider yourself more spiritual than religious, you can meet a number of like-minded, interested users.

Do you imagine that your encounters with Christian singles will be less than exciting? Christians are not shut-ins, everyone has hobbies and interest from super-active and busy, to a more of a relaxed pace of activities. The trick is to find someone with a lifestyle that compliments yours.

Are Christians trying to live their lives to a somewhat higher standard? In most cases, yes. That's a good thing, especially when it comes to having those altruistic qualities that we all strive for, on one level or another.

Perhaps a date or possible mate, who is a bit more reserved and grounded, is just what you've been searching for, in all the wrong places.

Although a number of the big box dating sites list the sites on the Christian dating list. It's more like twisting data for marketing purposes. Many of the dating sites have a question related to religious preference. So based on the one question, the website has a search option to search by any category. Big box dating sites uses this data to mislabel its site as Christian, to solicit niche site users.

Match dot com, Zoosk dot com and eHarmony, list its sites as Christian. Not even close. Make sure you use a clearly Christian based site, if it is your preference.

Cleanup some of the shallow language in your current online dating profile, used to sometimes entice the wrong type of people; and post a page on a Christian dating site. Try something new, after all that's why you started online dating in the first place.

Part Four: Personal Preferences Shallow and Non-Shallow

Women and Men who lie about their age

Since when is it a disgrace to grow old gracefully? The topic of age can be a touchy subject for some. Sadly, something as common as a simple question of a person's age can immediately put some people on the defensive, while others blurt it out without a second thought.

Asking a women her age is considered bad form and downright rude to most women over age-40. So what's the problem for some people when it comes to divulging their age? The answer is simple. Labeling. In our youth oriented society women and men of a certain age are considered past 'their prime.' A sad state of affairs for those youthful 40+ souls, who are attractive, fit, fabulous, and whose appearance is that of a person, considerably younger than what their accumulative birthdays denote.

When you feel that you have quite a lot of living to do, and achieving your dreams, and realizing your ambitions, are on the horizon for you, and then you are shut down to a degree socially, because of you age! This is a bone of contention, and rightfully so.

Albeit, women have been lying about their age for ages. In the online dating arena it is a red flag, and considered deceptive. Now, men are getting in on the act of concealing their age. Is fibbing about your age a little white lie or major deception? If you meet a possible mate who wants a family, a 10-year younger fib by a women of age-50, can be a deal-breaker for a hopeful family man. Besides, if someone will lie about something so minor; what else will he or she lie about? The reasons for lying about one's true age varies, but none of it is justifiable. The cause may stem from any one or more of the following:

If a man wants to date a 25-year-old woman and he's age 45; depending on the woman, she may perceive him as more of a 'Dad' type, than a love interest. By listing his age as 35, there is still a sizable age gap of 10-years, but it may be more palatable to the woman than a 20-year age gap.

On the flip-side, women lie about their age to escape being labeled and overlooked online. While older men are busy chasing after younger women, there are slightly older and sultry women available. The good news is, these slightly older, attractive women can date younger men and feel totally comfortable and confident about it. Cougars 1, Age Oppression 0.

Lying about your age is not cool. Put yourself in the other person's position. Imagine if you are a man or woman, and you're seeing a person whom you are very fond of and the feelings are mutual. The coupling progresses to an intimate relationship, but you still have not confessed your age deception? To hear from you or find out elsewhere of a 10-15-year age difference could be devastating. If you are hoping that it really doesn't matter because now he or she has feelings for you? Your partner may feel totally misled, betrayed and angry.

I find that a lot of people look younger than their actual age. So why not just be happy with the fact that you look great and feel great. If you allow dated notions and stereotypes related to age, to affect your self-esteem, then you are belittling yourself and not being true to the awesome person that you are.

Are children a deal breaker?

In the online dating world you can select options related to what sort of relationship arrangement you are seeking. Based on your preconceived notions of interest, you convey your needs for a relationship at this stage in your life. These indications also act as helpful clues to others who are seeking the same things. You decide if you are seeking; casual dating, long term, friends, intimate encounters, or marriage. There are also options regarding your preferences related to having children; yes, no, undecided/open, or already have.

Essentially, in reading an online dating profile, you can discern in five minutes of reading, what another person's position is on relationships, marriage and children. Otherwise it could take months of getting to know a person to find out about his or her disposition on the topic. It's quite a nifty time saver.

You set-up your online profile and you decide to select "long term to marriage" and you say yes to wanting children. Okay, great but what's driving you to settle down in a committed relationship? Why now? Is it a romantic notion of true love and finding your soul's counterpart and spending the rest of your life blissfully happy and in love? Sounds good. I certainly hope it's what is driving you? Or it is simply an inclination of it's "about that time" for you to settle down?

You'd should really stop and think, and fully realize the implications of your choices before you venture on to an ultimately disastrous path. Not just for you, but for others who may be depending on you for the long haul.

A ticking biological clock is not a stable reason for rushing headlong into marriage and having children. Real love is worth waiting for at any age or at any stage in your life.

Now let's talk a bit about marriage and having children as it pertains to cultural and social norms. In certain cultures, if you are over age 30 and still unmarried without children, male or female, it's a cause for concern and disapproval within the family structure and within the culture. It's not merely a cultural aspect; there are societal norms associated with getting married and having children. It's biblical, traditional and the natural course of things in life. Right?

So what about those individuals who don't want to have children, ever? Where does it leave them? Will you stand your ground and be honest with yourself about your true desires; or will you cave in and settle for a husband or wife and a life, that's not a life, it's an existence, a routine, settled for by you, because it's about that time? Are you living your life the way you want to? Or are you doing what is expected of you at this station in life? Try to grasp the difference.

Although it is natural to love, support and protect children. The thought of watching a two-year-old run around the floor in circles for hours, day and night, may be too mind numbing for some to consider. For others it's a "seemingly" great life, this condition of parenthood. Great life, or enthusiastically tolerated routine? Some people don't know the difference; I would imagine it's a lot easier this way.

The pros and cons of parenthood are vast in scope. However, it's a matter of choice and like marriage it's not a decision to be entered into lightly. The choice to have children or not, is very personal. It does not require any explanation or justification to anyone, whichever the decision.

If you don't want children you simply need to find a mate who shares your position. If you decide that you want children? Is the desire to have children a primary reason to move forward to marriage? Being in love is the quintessential reason for marriage and then sharing that love with children at some point. Children born into loveless marriages of convenience or opportunity could be affected in a negative way.

Parents are the greatest role model for children in the formative years. A loving, passionate and affectionate relationship shared between the child's parents, or a lukewarm, distant, dispassionate relationship. I'm afraid "polite pleasantries" are no substitution for love. So you spoil the kids rotten and coddle them to no end in an effort to over compensate. You wrap your life around them, making sure that they feel loved. But do you feel loved?

Children "need you" for the most part and eventually learn to "love you." In a loveless marriage, is being "needed" by children a comparable substitute for being loved?

A loveless marriage of timing for the sake of procreating is horribly selfish and unfair to the children born of such a union. A child deserves a loving family relationship. You are not only short changing the children, you are short changing yourself. People wed for reasons other than love. They make the choice, and the children suffer the consequences.

Without a strong foundation of love to support a marriage, along with passion, mutual respect and compatibility, you are biding time until the marriage eventually unravels, due to the lack of these qualities. Divorce and broken homes have become a cliché in the U.S., as the divorce rate holds steadily at 50% of marriages ending in divorce. The U.S. as a country has the highest divorce rate worldwide. It is number one in divorce rate, but not number one in population. In comparison to other countries with considerably more citizens, yet lower divorce rates; this equates to an astronomical number of people in the U.S., consistently making poor decisions in marriage.

On a happier note, to all of you hopeful singles out there optimistically holding out for the real deal, I applaud and salute you. Follow your heart for however long it takes. Be happy and productive and enjoy life in the moment. Choose a husband or wife for the right reason, choose love. It's worth it and you may actually find it online. Fact: Marriages via online dating are steadily on the rise, but you have to hang in there.

A larger number of people, who are divorced with children, and starting over in the dating pool, are infiltrating the online dating world. Singles with no children, will need to decide if dating a divorcee with children is right for you.

Are you considering dating a divorcee with children? How can you not be, they seem to be everywhere. In the world of online dating you'll notice the "divorced" status listed on profile after profile. This is especially true in the age range of 35-50+. There are a few things to consider before you decide to date someone with a failed marriage or two under their belt. And if there are children involved? I'll tell you straight out, the cons may outweigh the pros.

Does this seem unfair to the divorcees? Are we judging people based on their situation and not really knowing them personally? Yes. Why? Because depending on how badly their marriage ended and all of the emotionality connected to the ordeal, and it is an ordeal.

A failed marriage experience can taint their outlook on love, marriage and relationships in general.

Do we really want to date people with unresolved issues, anger, obsession, bitterness, emotional damage, and animosity linked to their failed marriage? Don't get me wrong, everyone deserves a loving relationship. Unfortunately, everyone is not functional and capable of maintaining a healthy, loving relationship.

Example: A divorced Mom will be extra cautious in dating; going to great lengths to make certain that she can trust you, as it pertains to being around her children. While it is understandable that she is protective of her children, but is it fair to a man to undergo excessive scrutiny because of a divorced Mom's fears and uncertainties?

You are trying to get to know her and she is keeping you at arm's length out of a fear that has nothing to do with you personally. If you dated a single woman without children, this element could be considerably less excessive. It's a bit different for women dating a divorced Dad, who has shared custody. The children are usually around him on the weekend, which incidentally may be the time when you are hoping to make plans with him for dating and events.

On the topic of divorced men, I say beware of newly divorced men who are not necessarily looking for a relationship. HELLO! He just got out of a relationship. More than likely they are looking for sexual conquest, while being less than forthcoming about their true intentions.

Female and male, divorced parents have no problem telling their potential dates that their kids come first in their life. Yes, their children should come first in their life, agreed. However, as a single person without children, a divorced parent's priority of their children first, is not your priority nor your problem. Unless of course you decide to be involved in their life. If so, be prepared to take the backseat when it comes to their children. Now if the backseat is a less than ideal position for you in a relationship? I suggest you make an effort to date singles, without children.

Divorced parents have additional stress factors related to childrearing that don't exist for singles, without children. Is a relationship with a single, without children easier based on this aspect? No, there are no guarantees when it comes to relationships. Relationships are never completely simple and there is always some degree of compromise. My best tip in this situation is following your heart, but use your head.

Some people are more compassionate, supportive and patient than others, these are great qualities in a mate, and ideal qualities when it comes to dating a divorced parent. As for some, prefer ease and simplicity over complications whenever possible.

In the case of divorced parents, don't take it personally if you find that some people are a little skittish. You made a happy decision to have children so don't be offended that others don't want to be involved. It's not about people being selfish, it's about people making active choices.

My best tip and rule of thumb to anyone considering dating a divorcee, is do not date him or her if they are divorced less than one year minimum, and I'm being very liberal at one year. The longer time divorced the better.

When dating a divorcee, if you notice that a lot of their conversation is about their former spouse and failed marriage? Head for the hills! You don't need to be a sounding board for their need to vent, obsess, or rationalize their past relationship failures. That's what a therapist is for. If you do pass the safety clearance, and are included in family outings with the children, refrain from any comments related to the children's behavior. Some parents are notoriously in denial about their little angels' habits. For the most part, children are only really tolerable to their parents and family, educators and childcare workers, e.g. people who get "paid" to deal with them.

The truth so refreshing! But then again, there are those very special children, who are so delightful, funny, adorable, sweet, or talented, that they simply melt your heart. Naturally, all parents think that their children are the latter.
The day that parents accept the fact that their children have bad behavior problems, the sooner they can help their child development proper and appropriate behavior. It's much easier to ignore the problem and let the children run wild, to avoid the confrontations and avoid actually having to apply parenting skills.

Wouldn't it be easier if singles stick with singles and divorcees stick with the same? I was lucky enough to have one of the greatest step-father on the planet. Bottom line, it's your choice, but remembers if you are single and choose to date a divorced parent, be extremely patient, it could be worth it in the end.

Does race really matter?

What's your preference? What do you find appealing in the opposite sex and why? Does race play any role in your attraction? In the interest of social awareness, racial tolerance and inclusion; we know that treating all people equally is the right thing to do. How far are you willing to go in your beliefs?

Would you consider marrying someone outside of your race? The great melting pot of multi-ethnicities and race mixing has created a new fusion of biracial and multiracial women and men. The racial lines are segued by the influx of these multi-nationalities. In their case, is race a disposition or persuasion, an active choice, and no longer a dated assignment by skin color?

The bottom line is attraction. Physical, intellectual, common interest and chemistry. If you can truly accept a person without regard to race? Congratulations! You have reached the next plateau of the truly evolved mind. If you place race limitations on your search for a soulmate, you narrow the field of selection to match your narrow vision.

Sex with no strings attached

To abstain or not to abstain, that is the question? Whether 'tis nobler in the mind to suffer the slings and arrows of cheap, tawdry sex, while in search of a suitable mate.

What role does sex play in the dating process? Sex on the second date, fifth date or tenth date? When is the time right? Those self-proclaimed free spirits, whom maintain a fervent belief in "going with the flow and living in the moment", might lead you to believe that a random sex act with someone you barely know is fun, sexy and spontaneous! Well, I guess that's one way to look at it.

On the other hand, some may view this behavior as promiscuous, immoral and desperate. Is there a middle ground? Not really. A sexual encounter stemming from boredom, loneliness or for the sake of the sex act itself, is definitely not sexy.

Feigned emotion and contrived passion is an affront to one's own emotionality. Sex with no strings e.g. no attachment or 'Friends with benefits,' another reference used to describe a casual sex partner, is nothing but a cheap, illusory, poor substitute for a loving, functional relationship.

For those who find this arrangement suitable as a means to relieve sexual tension or quell sexual desires, you are on a slippery slope to losing the true essence of intimacy, by trading love and true intimacy for a perfunctory sex act. While granted consenting adults have the right to conduct their sex lives as they choose. Choose better!

By exercising a healthy dose of self-esteem and self-control, you'll find that holding out for the real thing, is a hell of a lot sexier when you find it.
Besides if you don't have the patience and self-control to wait, I can almost guarantee you'll never find it. Hence your current predicament of choice.

A messy sex life intertwined with friends who are also casual sex partners can prove to be very awkward when transitioning to a healthy, functional, loving relationship with someone special.

A male or female who has casual sex with friends or an ex-partner, while professing that they are single, is being deceptive, and may find that this sort of deceitful behavior is a "deal breaker" to a new love interest.

Fit or Fat - What is your true body type?

Athletic, Average, Slim, Thin, A few extra pounds, BBW, Curvy, Stocky, or Portly? These are common body type descriptions used on various online dating websites. The issue with these self-applied body labels in the online dating arena is the descriptions are somewhat subjective.

If a woman describes her body type as "a few extra pounds" and she is in fact obese and 40 pounds over the appropriate weight for her measured height, she is clearly being misleading and lying about her body type.

A few extra pounds by definition, has a cut-off at less than 10 pounds above your correct height/weight ratio. If your body weight is within the appropriate height/weight ratio, then your body type is average.

So why bother lying? Pride, ego, denial, people want to save face online? I guess "a few extra pounds" sounds better than "morbidly obese."

The same type of bending the truth, applies in the body type descriptions of "athletic" and "average." A man who is 40 pounds overweight but exercises twice a week, labels himself as "athletic," based on a minor fitness routine. If you work-out twice a week, but you eat 20% of your body weight in cheeseburgers and chili cheese fries, 7-days a week, hence the extra 40 pounds, you do not have an athletic physique.

For research, and contacting several very attractive men on various popular dating websites, I selected users with a very specific statement notated in their online dating profiles. All of the men made comments about receiving email messages from "fat" women. The men also incorporated a note to "fat women" in their profiles, clearly stating that they are not interested in meeting women who are overweight.

Why would women who are clearly overweight, obese, etc., email message the hottest and most fit guys on the dating site? What are these women thinking? I would imagine that they are thinking what many women think. There is more to them than just their body and looks. The same statement can apply to any woman of any body type, and any person, female or male.

Nevertheless, let's keep it honest people. In the event that you don't have the body of a Supermodel or Herculean Adonis, and you don't feel comfortable labeling yourself, you can select the "prefer not to say" or "no answer" options in the body type listing on the dating profile. You should also post a current, full body picture on your dating profile page. By doing this, you are clearly showing, what you see, is what you get, no label required.

Height Stereotype - Is taller better?

If you happen to notice a tall attractive woman holding hands and walking with a much shorter, average looking man, what is your first impression? Do you glance at them and think nothing, or do you immediately attach labels? "He must be rich and she must be a gold digger." "How does a guy like him get a woman like her?" "She's totally out of his league." Or perhaps you slyly snicker at the seemingly awkward, mismatched duo. The fact is these two are probably not concerned about height stereotypes.

In the U.S. taller men have better jobs, more success with women, and more money than their shorter counterparts. This according to Malcom Gladwell in his book "Blink: The Power of Thinking without Thinking," a New York Times bestseller. For his book, Gladwell polled about half of the Fortune 500 companies and found that the majority of their CEOs were tall, white men.

The average CEO was just under 6' feet (the average American man is 5'9")

Among the CEOs, 58 percent were 6' feet or over

In the United States, 14.5 percent of men are 6' feet or over

Some 30 percent of the CEOs were 6'2" or taller

Only 3.9 percent of U.S. men are 6'2" or taller

Women in general prefer taller men, at least 4-6 inches taller than she, according to several Matchmaker style, dating services. Not to be confused with online dating services. Daters who choose Matchmaker service don't hunt and peck online.

They give a list of needs to the Matchmaker service and the leg work is done by the service. When women give their list, "tall" is usually at, or near the top.

There is an element of sexiness associated with a very tall, fit, attractive man. They seem bigger, stronger and more masculine and protective than short men. Not always true on the stronger side. I've been very surprised by how much weight an average or shorter than average man can lift, in a gym setting. In some cases more than double his weight. Does it seem trivial and shallow to let a few inches in height stand between you and the possibility of love?

It's true, a great deal of women do not prefer men who are shorter than she. The height dynamic works both ways. A man of average height at 5'9, who normally dates women between 5'2-5'5, will cower when face to face with a woman who is 5'9 and wearing three inch heels, equaling a total height of 6'.

He looks shorter and sometimes feels short next to her, even though they are both the same height. This can be a little awkward for both partners. The only thing to be said in his case is be securing with who you are, and stop letting petty insecurities, and other people's perceived opinions, affect your choices and feelings. However, if tall is truly your preference? You can perform a custom search on most dating sites and specify a height minimum in your search. Or you can try a niche dating site that caters strictly to tall singles.

Dating and Fitness - When a few extra pounds are a few too many

In a conducted online dating experiment, using a single, identical head shot photo, posted on two online dating websites, with all profile details identical, except one.

One profile listed the female subject's body description as "a few extra pounds," and the other listed the body type as "athletic."

The profile with the body type listed as "athletic" received seven times more responses than the profile listed as "a few extra pounds." Additionally, the male suitors who responded to the popular profile were considerably more attractive and fit in their profile photos.

People are naturally attracted to the well-defined physique. The sight of sculpted Abs or the curvaceous derriere of your favorite actor or singer can make your heart skip a beat. While beauty is subjective, and in the eye of the beholder to coin the old adage, there are some universal standards of attraction that command attention.

The fact of the matter is people who are very fit and attractive, in most cases, are seeking the same in a counterpart. If you are overweight in relation to your height and body frame, but you feel comfortable in your skin, great! But for health purposes taking action to improve your overall fitness can be beneficial in the long run.

If you are less than fit, but are attracted to the hard body types, don't be too disappointed if you don't receive a response. It doesn't necessarily indicate that the person is shallow, but they may have a fitness lifestyle that is important to them, and they want the same in a partner. This is completely fair. If you are a major fitness enthusiast, you may want to consider a niche dating site geared strictly towards the fitness minded. Dating sites like FitnessSingles dot com or Fitness Date Club dot com.

Age stereotype - Should women hide their age?

In a society geared towards youth, double standards and ageism between the sexes is still very active. Will stereotypes, discrimination and double standards ever end in a decent society? Is true equality a lofty illusion that we aspire to, or is it achievable in small doses?

In the dating process there are many singling out factors used to narrow the field, and age is one of those factors.

In the dating world, does singling out individuals based on their age, a form of discrimination? It certainly is in the professional world. This is the primary reason for established laws to protect persons over age-40, from hiring discrimination.

Have you ever met someone that you really liked as a person, but felt that the age difference may be less than ideal, or worse a deal breaker?

Any woman at any age, who enjoys fitness and chooses a healthy lifestyle, may have good health advantages. Add great genetics as measured by one's appearance in relation to one's age, and these factors may further enhance a "youthful" appearance.

Political correctness aside, bottom line some women look younger than what their true age implies. Is this fact a license to fudge the truth about one's age? More often than not, when you ask someone their age in any setting, other than for health or professional purposes, the immediate answer is usually the question; "How old do I look?"

After all what are the reasons for asking someone their age in any other scenario other than for labeling purposes. In our society being labelled as a woman over 40, can actually diminish your dating circle.

The popular dating site Match dot com examined the reasons why some older men prefer to date younger women. Okay. So what about older women who prefer to date younger men?

The differences of opinions are quite the polar opposite. Men claim that younger women are readily single and available while women their own age are married, divorced or in the process of divorcing.

This leads to the second reason why older men prefer younger women. Less emotional baggage. Men also view younger as free spirited and depending on how young the woman is she may be less likely to want to settle down right away, making her the perfect target for men looking for a more carefree relationship without strings.

An ego stroke may play a role for some men, feeling that attracting a younger woman makes them "feel" younger and more desirable.

Older women with more life experience and career experience may have more success than their younger counterparts. Older men on the Match dot com survey felt that younger women are easier to impress compared to women their own age.

In some cases women over 40 who hide their age are faced with a dilemma. Conceal their age in order to expand the number of men in their dating pool, or be forthcoming about their age and take what they can get, in this case whoever is interested in her particular age demographic. Keeping in mind that a number of the men in her age range are seeking younger women.

Bottom line, lying about your age to deceive someone can backfire. If you develop feelings for the person you must tell him the truth and risk being rejected. If you are banking on the man developing feelings for you, and he won't care about your age, you could be in for a rude awakening with hurt feeling all around. Embrace who you are and what you have accomplished. Starting a relationship based on any lie could destroy a potentially promising romance.

Part Five: Online Dating Etiquette
Who's paying?

Attractive, fit, sexy, intelligent and gainfully employed. Is this too much to ask for in dating? At times, it appears so. More often than not one or more of these highly desirable qualities seem to missing in potential suitors, and you may be in for a lot of dates that lead nowhere.

Attractiveness is somewhat subjective, but there are a few universal aesthetics which set the standards for beauty and sex appeal, notwithstanding one's own individual taste.

Good fitness is a necessity, not just for sex appeal but for a comfort level and healthy lifestyle. As for gainful employment, in this economy and fluctuating job market what jobs are even safe now? White-collar or Blue-collar? Even with these factors we still have certain expectations and standards in our dating needs.

If you were downsized from a company and have to take a lower paying job, this can wreak havoc on your personal finances which includes your entertainment budget. And what if you are just flat-out unemployed and diligently seeking employment at the same or similar level of your previous job? Does this mean that you should put your social life on hold until your financial situation changes?

Yes, there is still somewhat of a negative stigma of failure connected to being unemployed, especially for men who are unemployed. So as a man, if your funds are low, is it okay to ask your date to share in a small part of the expense?

In general, women are not accustomed to paying and they don't really need to pay. And if you can't afford to pay for the date expenses then she can go out with someone else who can afford it. Remember, she doesn't really know you too well and she doesn't need to make concessions around your financial "situation".

However, some women are more relaxed about chipping in and it's not a problem, down the line. But on the first date? Plan to pay guys and then feel out the shared expenses situation first, as not to embarrass yourself and give the impression of being ill-bred and unchivalrous, not to mention cheap or broke.

There are fun and cost effective date

options. Offering to cook for your date is generally well received. A nice pasta meal, garlic bread, a bottle of vino, even you can handle that? A cocktail happy hour with discounted appetizers and cocktails and then a romantic walk. A quiet picnic with deli sandwiches, cranberry coleslaw, a bottle of wine, sparkling conversation and you. What more can a girl ask for?

How to deal with negative and toxic people

According to Forbes.com online dating sites are posting revenues in excess of 400% plus, year upon year. More and more single and divorced men and women are joining the ranks of the online dating community.

If you live in a major city the numbers of profiles on a popular dating site are overwhelming in the sheer volume alone. If you live in a small town you may find more undesirable profiles based on an overall limited selection. Trust me; if you see a gem on a dating site with less traffic, you better believe that lots of hopeful daters are in pursuit this person.

If you're a particularly attractive woman or man, you may be faced with a relentless onslaught of responders. Sounds great right? More choices? Not so much. Unfortunately all of your responders are not necessarily admirers. Some of them may be downright rude and insulting, and desperate, and demonstrably unattractive. So why would someone take the time to contact you just to insult you in the process?

Toxic people in general, male or female,

derive some sort of satisfaction in attacking others verbally. They need an outlet in which to direct their negative views and attitude. It could be a friend, co-worker, family member or a complete stranger. It has nothing to do with you; it's their way of spreading negativity. These people seek any reason to be negative towards others even if they have to create a reason in their own mind.

There's no need to contemplate the psychological pathology of these misguided souls. The easy answer may be jealousy. Everyone else likes you and thinks you are super attractive, but toxic people try to insult you, this allows them some pathetic sense of distinction in being the one who doesn't like you.

Unbeknownst to the toxic personality type, their negative feelings only affect them, not you. So what is the best way to deal with this sort of person, in online dating? Frankly there is no need, this person's rude insults or unsubstantiated dislike for you does not affect you one bit. You are still wonderful, and there's nothing that anyone can say that will change the facts. Never respond to a toxic troll. They don't deserve your attention for their inappropriate behavior.

Of course if you receive vulgar or explicit messages from anyone, almost every dating site has a reporting, or blocking feature. You can block the user or report the email message and the user can be banned from the site, accordingly.

As a selective but cordial online user, how do you weed-out the undesirables, e.g. people that you have no interest in meeting, without appearing unkind or shallow?

Weeding out the undesirable candidates, and targeting the most suitable ones in a vast sea of online dating responders, can be time consuming and tedious. It seems the polite thing to do when someone sends you an email message of interest, and you are not interested, is to respond and politely decline. Never do this!

Email messaging people who you are not interested is even more time consuming, and you will likely receive additional email messages once you respond. You can't spend your days or evenings responding to excessive email messages.

If you are short on time and want to target your search to those who you find better suited, the best way to do this is to be very specific in your description of what you are seeking in a mate. Don't be afraid of appearing too shallow, too picky or limiting your number of responses. If you describe a very specific type of mate, you will at least reduce the number of responders who don't fit the description of attributes.

Let's face it, the first thing we notice in a person's dating profile is the photo. Depending on your personal taste and what you find attractive; you either look further and read-on, or skip to the next profile or email message. It's just like in real life; we notice a person's appearance first. It's not about being shallow, you either find someone attractive or you don't in some cases.

However, attraction can grow over time. It absolutely can, just as love, respect and affection for a person can grow over time. On that note, just before passing on those dating profile photos that were marginal in physical attractiveness, you just might want to take a second look every now and then.

Dealing with rejection

In the online dating arena rejection is par for the course. You may be rejected, or reject others, it goes both ways. When seeking a potential mate, the important thing to remember is it's a process. If there's an initial interest in the person prior to meeting, based on good communication and similar interest, and then after meeting, you find that there is no chemistry. How do you proceed?

We naturally click with some people better than with others, but it's important to take the time to try to get know someone over time, to see what develops. If you decide after only one date that you have no continued interest, and it happens. Be kind, tactful and honest in letting your date know where you stand. Hiding your real feelings and silently bowing out without a word is inconsiderate.

The best way to do this is to first tell your date what you like about him or her. Think in terms of the positive things that compelled you to make the date. You should follow-up by letting your date know that you want to continue the dating process and meet additional dating interest. You should also express thanks for the opportunity to meet and spend some time together.

If you are the one rejected, remember to be mature and try not to take it too personally. Don't press the issue or demand more answers. Just like your date have other options, so do you. You'll be out having fun on your next date in no time.

Exit strategies for dead-end relationships

When it comes to dating and relationships there are two common mistakes. One is not picking the right person for you, in the long run. The other is not getting out quickly enough after realizing the mismatch.

I am all for giving someone a chance and taking the time to assess the possibilities of a potential relationship. However, if in the process it is determined that the relationship has too many dysfunctional aspects to continue for the long-term, it's best to move on swiftly. Accepting a less than suitable partner out of neediness, settling, or comfort zone, is a surefire recipe for a regretfully time wasting, relationship experience.

Suffice to say if you are in a relationship whereas you and your partner are on different pages, in the classification of the relationship, you could be time to move on. For example, you want a long-term relationship and marriage, and he or she doesn't (not with you.)

Generally speaking, should couples continue in relationships of comfort with no intention of marriage? If so, for how long?

If you can, it's best to determine sooner rather than later, the true intentions of your partner. If you finally come to the conclusion that the relationship is not heading in your desired direction, suggesting an open relationship and dating other people, would be a turning point for the relationship, one way or the other.

If a clean break is your preference, the truth is effective in stating that "we" seem to be in "different stages" in our relationship needs, and I think that we should explore other options.

Part Six: Single for the Holidays and Valentine's Day

A Singleton's guide to holiday fun

Whether its holiday parties, family gatherings or waking up on Christmas morning to an empty bed, the holidays are sometimes a stark reminder, conjuring up those feeling of need, in not having a special love interest to share in these sentimental moments. If you are unattached and feeling a bit isolated and hesitant to attend holiday functions unaccompanied, I say to you, get over it!

Christmas is a wonderful holiday, filled with cheer, festivities, warmth, spiritual and religious significance (for Christians) and PRESENTS. You should in no way dismiss, hide out or feel slighted during the holiday season because you don't have a significant other, at the time.

On the contrary, you should have as much fun as you can, as always. The fact that you are single should not even be a consideration.

If you are just coming off of a bad break-up, try to keep your focus on the New Year ahead, and all of the exciting possibilities that a fresh start will bring. Don't linger, dwell or obsess about the past.

Even if the thoughts of the past are at times, warm and happy, keep them in perspective and look beyond those thoughts to more happiness in the future. But, if the thoughts are emotionally hurtful, why do it? Why reflect on things that are negative or hurtful to you?

In dealing with the break-up of a love relationship, my motto is move on and don't look back, unless there is a reason to smile in a brief moment's reflection, and that's it, a moment.

For holiday fun, find your Plus-one. If you are not familiar with the Plus-one reference, it is defined as: "a person who accompanies an invited guest to a social function".

Plus-one is not defined as a date; it can be a male, female, friend, family member, co-worker etc. If you don't have a romantic interest to invite to a party, don't skip the event, make some phone calls.

See who is free and ask them if he or she will be your Plus-one? Call your friends, male or female, siblings, co-worker, and a nice neighbor in your building complex. There are lots of possibilities.

You're inviting them to a fun party to have a good time, not to the dentist. Someone will certainly take you up on your cordial invite. By the way, you can invite your dentist to be your Plus-one. Now that we have covered the bases on holiday parties and family gatherings, let's cover the fun Christmas morning.

If you must wake-up to an empty bed, make it the most wonderful, luxurious bed ever. Splurge on red satin sheets and satin throw pillows. Buy yourself a sexy red negligee or red silk pajamas for the guys.

Place a basket on your bed side table, filled with pine cones purchased from your neighborhood florist; add cinnamon sticks and apple potpourri, or that new Christmas smell. If you don't like the shopping mall during the holidays, buy these items on Amazon or EBay and have it delivered to your door. You're worth it.

It's Christmas morning; don't settle for your standard breakfast cereal. Make a special and hearty breakfast for yourself. Pancakes with fresh fruit and whipped cream, eggs, bacon, sausage. If you don't know how to make pancakes or can't cook to save your life? Pop some frozen waffles in the toaster and add strawberry syrup, fresh strawberries, banana slices and whipped cream.

Otherwise spend your day calling or visiting relatives, trimming the tree, watching the holiday programs, parades, football bowl games. Drink spiked eggnog with gingerbread cookies, or do whatever you want? Anyway, its one day and then it's all over, so why not enjoy it, and make it the best.

Out of the box Valentine's Day for Singles

The countdown to Valentine's Day starts in January. It's when the retailers flood the department stores with hokey love paraphernalia. Dinner reservations have to be made weeks in advance, as a standard. The cost of roses triples, and be prepared to make a trip to the jewelry store, if roses or chocolates just won't cut it.

Whether you are single, in a long-term relationship, or just recently met someone new, Valentine's Day beckons for attention. So here are some ideas for Valentine's Day fun, whether you are attached or single for the day.

1. Be a tourist in your own city. Consider what makes your city great and attracts tourist. Museums, photo or art galleries, local points of interest, historical landmarks, and any popular tourist attractions will do. Go out to these places and enjoy the scene. If you are single, once you're out having fun, Valentine's Day becomes just another fun day.

2. Take a cooking class. Even the best cooks can always pick-up some pointers from a Pro. If your cooking skills are average, look

at it as a good chance to improve, or learn how to prepare unique or exotic meals.

3. Listen to live music. Check out local clubs or bars offering live rock, jazz or karaoke events. Hang-out and enjoy the music, and if the mood strikes you? Go on stage and sing your favorite songs, which make you smile.

4. Take a dance lesson. Check in your town for a local dance studio that offers, Salsa, Country line, or Hip-hop, dance lessons. Country line dancing lessons are great; you can dance on your own in a group, or be pared with a partner in class.

5. No date for V-Day, have an impromptu party. Invite every single or divorced friend, co-worker or neighbor, to a pot-luck event. Everyone can bring whatever they choose. Just add wine and soft-drinks and you have a very cool and easy Valentine's Day soiree.

Why Saint Patrick's Day is more fun for singles

You don't need to be Irish to enjoy Saint Patrick's Day. Although the highly celebrated day has a "sober" history, pun intended. Looking at the lighter side of the day is not uncommon in the U.S.

Saint Patrick's Day is celebrated on March 17th. It began as a religious feast day for the patron saint of Ireland and has become an international festival celebrating Irish culture. The Irish have observed this day as a religious holiday for over 1,000 years.

With all of the parties at bars and pubs, street carnivals and parades, it's a great opportunity to meet new people, have some cool cocktails and tasty grinds with up-to-date recipes on the traditional corn beef and cabbage meal. Corn beef and cabbage pizza, and crispy Asian-style corn beef and cabbage spring rolls, are creative takes on the classic.

Ice cold green beer and green cocktails are all the rage for St. Patrick's Day. A number of pubs serve green beer, and other green drinks to consider in keeping with the day's green theme. You might want to try a Melon

Ball or Apple Martini. Here's one of my own favorite special drinks with a twist.

"Peppermint Paddy"
One part Green Crème de Menthe
One part White Crème de Cacao
One part Vanilla Vodka
Add half & half cream, and shake briskly over ice
Garnish with a chocolate chips

St. Patrick's Day parties are a must, drink in moderation, and take a half-day off of work in advance, for the after, provided you have the vacation time or a flexible work schedule. It's worth it. Check your local newspaper to find parties in your area. Assign a designated driver or use a car service for the evening.

St. Patrick's Day parades are colorful and great fun. Check your local area newspaper for parades or festivals. In 1762 in New York City, the first parade honoring this holiday took place. To today the record stands as the largest celebration and parade in the U.S. Almost 3 million people attend the festivities. Remember Saint Patrick's Day is to singles, what Valentine's Day is to couples. Get your green on, and don't miss out on the fun.

Part Seven: Dating Slump and Starting Over

Breaking the dating slump

You create a snazzy online dating profile using your most amazing pics. You write a profile descriptive and it's witty and intelligent. You receive tons of responses and have some pretty fun dates in the process. After a while the interest in your dating profile diminishes. You are now receiving little to no responses.

This happens sometimes when your profile has been online for a good while and there are not many new subscribers who fit your preferences, joining the dating site. It's like when you search for new dating prospect and see the same old faces.

There are a few things you can do in this case. Post new pics and refresh your profile descriptive, join another paid dating site with hopefully new prospects, or hide your profile for a while and take a mini-break from the online dating scene.

I recommend joining a free Meetup group in your local area. This is a great way to meet new friends, enjoy group outings, and enjoy some real-time interactions.

Perhaps at one of the group outings you may meet someone terrific, outside of the group. There is life outside of online dating, and sometimes you can have the best of both worlds in your search for "The One."

Starting over after age 50

Till death do us part; a declaration of undying love. The idea of eternal love transcends the reality of selecting a mate for life, and maintaining a never-ending interest in the relationship. Personal growth, new interest, lifestyle changes, and a lackluster sex life, can contribute to changing taste.

Consistently working at improving a stale marriage and finding ways to be happy with your mate can pacify or prolong the inevitable realization that you have outgrown the relationship. Is companionship, and being comfortable in a relationship, enough to hang in there?

Sometimes you have to face the music, and call it quits. The turmoil, mixed emotions, the legal obligations, separation of property and the feeling of losing your best friend. This doesn't really even begin to scratch the surface. And if there are children involved, it is especially devastating.

Divorce rates for people over age 50, has doubled. There were around 300,000 couples in the U.S., over the age 50, who divorced in 2008. Researchers at Bowling Green State University in Kentucky have recently released a compilation of statistics that looked at the divorce rate for American couples over 50 years of age.

The starting point for this analysis was 1990, and at that time the divorce rate for people of this age group was 4.67 divorces for every 1,000 people. However, in 2008, the divorce rate had risen to 9.74 per 1,000 people, or more than doubles the rate 18 years earlier.

The baby boomers are on their 2nd or 3rd divorces. It is suggested that their strong values and belief in the institution of marriage spurs them on to re-marry after multiple failed marriages. No matter how many failed marriages, or relationships that one person has, the search for love and companionship continues. There is no good reason, to give up on love.

Online dating is a great game plan for getting back into the dating scene after a divorce is final, and waiting at least one year or longer to start perusing new companions. In using online dating you can find a date within your appropriate age group without hanging around singles bars, which can be awkward for some.

Whether you are male or female, and your preference is to date someone younger than you are; online dating is ideal, as the subscribers offer a dating age range of interest. All online profiles offer the option of adding an age range as a dating preference. You can easily identify women or men who are interested in dating someone older. Make sure to always check for an age preference on a profile and respect the wishes of the user, if you are older than the age range specified. In the dating scene, anytime that you choose to approach the opposite sex to express interest, you can never be sure if the age difference is a deal breaker. And not everyone is polite when it comes to older men or women approaching them as a romantic interest. You don't want to embarrass yourself and appear undignified or lecherous.

Are you a serial dater?

Have you been involved in online dating for over a year? Over two years? Three to five years? If so you may be a serial dater.

While true, it may take some time to meet the right person. But, if you have been dating for years, and you are still hopelessly single with no real prospects for a long-term relationship, it may be time to pump the brakes. Take some time to examine your needs, experiences and true motives for remaining attached to online dating sites.

Dating is not a hobby or pastime. It should be treated as a fun and exciting means to an end, with some sort of intention in the process. It's primarily to establish a functional, long-term relationship.

If you are lingering on for years without a stable relationship, it's long overdue for you to take a look within yourself or your situation to find answers. If you are actually interested in a long-term relationship, and it is just not happening for you. Here are some things to consider:

1. Are you choosing dates for shallow reasons?

2. Are you disclosing "too much" information upfront and causing your dates to lose interest quickly?

3. Is your living arrangement not conducive to a one-on-one relationship? Live with parents, children, several roommates.

4. Are you unstable, financially or emotionally?

5. Are you're having sexual relations with your dates prematurely?

6. Are you seeking a mate who is out of your league? Attractiveness, education, finances?

7. Are you continuing to repeat the same failed pattern of dating habits?

Ask yourself introspective questions to see where changes in your approach or attitude can be made to help break the cycle of dead end dating.

Or seek advice from a trained psychologist, sometimes a third party perspective can shed some light on behaviors that may be self-sabotaging, or creating disconnects with others.

Part Eight: The Science of Dating

Why Blue Eyes are HOT

Blue eyes are most common in Ireland, the Baltic Sea area and Northern Europe. Blue eyes are also prominent in Eastern, Central, and Southern Europe.

Blue eyes are also found in parts of Western Asia, and most notably in Afghanistan, Syria, Iraq, and Iran, as well as among the Jewish population of Israel.

Genetics and multiracial integration e.g. individuals of mixed race heritage, on rare occasions, have natural blue eyes.

Now that we have established some of the origins of those gorgeous baby blues, let's talk about the sex appeal of blue eyes. What is the most common word association for the color blue? In Psychology the color blue is considered the overwhelming "favorite color."

Blue is seen as trustworthy, dependable, and committed. The color of the ocean and sky, blue is perceived as a constant in our lives. The color blue invokes restfulness and can have a calming effect on the body.

The calming effect of the color blue, the positive mental associations connected to the color, and the sexy X-factor that draws us in, all three may play a role in the sex appeal and allure.

While blond hair and blue eyes are very fair. Dark hair, tan skin and blue eyes, proves to be a very sexy and smoky alternative.

The Attachment Theory- Why some people suck and will die alone

The reference "long-term relationship" conjures up great and loving expectations for some people who think about how wonderful it is to have true love, and a committed partner in their life. Meanwhile there are others who feel fear and loathing at the very thought of a long-term relationship. Which one are you? And how many people have you met, who have an opposing view.

The Attachment Theory dissects personality types and identifies various attributes that determine how prone certain individuals will function in long-term relationships. There are groups of hopeful daters who struggle for lack of a better word, in finding a suitable partner. What are the underlined reasons why some people have challenges in finding a suitable and loving relationship? Or struggle in business relationships? Relationship attachment style can extend from personal to business relationships.

It's not exactly rocket science, having a loving well balanced relationship. It should be one of the most natural things ever. Why has dating, relationships and love become a challenge for some? Why does it take so much effort for some people to have a true loving relationship?

After 10-25 years of dating, failed relationships and one, two or three divorces, what is the real problem?

Friends, family members and strangers all seem to be on the same page in telling us that the reason for our lackluster love life is because "We haven't met the right person?"

Way to shift the blame to other people, instead of looking within ourselves to find out what is really going on? Yes, sometimes it is other people, but sometimes it's you! Take the time to look within, or stay in denial and keep repeating the same process and failing.

'I'm very picky" is another very popular excuse for why some people continue to fail at achieving something that should be completely natural. Maintaining a healthy, happy relationship, falling in love and getting married. That is, if marriage is your desire.

How long should one continue to cling to excuses before taking accountability and action in having a spectacular love life?

Relationship attachment types include: Secure, Anxious, Avoidant, with some slight variations between the styles. The relationship attachment style of your mate or potential mate can make or break the relationship, love affair or marriage in the long run, and especially in the beginning stages.

It's your relationship attachment style VS theirs, so it could be your own style causing the relationship breaking point, without you fully realizing what factors are in play.

The "Secure" relationship type is the healthiest, well-adjusted and arguably the one we should all strive for. The secure partner in relationship attachment science is a partner who is comfortable with closeness and intimacy in relationships and is usually consistent in their feelings and actions concerning their relationship.

A person with a secure attachment style may not be the most "exciting" for those drama kings and queens, but their straightforward and open manner creates a comfortable atmosphere and is an asset to the health and stability of a relationship.

Secure partner are luckily fairly common in

the population, reportedly one out of every two people has a secure relationship style. The bad news is that people with a secure style tend to find a partner early on and stay with them for a long time. So it may not be easy to find them. There are some out there though, and you may be one or be in a relationship with one.

Here are some signs of a potential secure partner that you may want to look out for:

1. Discusses plans and makes decisions with you

The partner with a secure attachment style will rarely make important decisions about the relationship by themselves. Instead they wait and ask for your input, and make decisions that take your views into account.

2. Does not believe relationships are hard work

Secure partners tend to be satisfied with their relationships, even during rough times. They don't dwell on small problems or talk about how difficult relationships are. They are open to starting a relationship even when their life circumstances or potential partner are not "perfect".

3. Trustworthy and reliable

When a person with a secure relationship
style says they will do something for you,
the chances are that they will. If they can't
follow through on a promise or plan they
made, they will explain why, usually in
advance.

4. Compromise

In disagreements secure partners like to
reach compromise. They are less concerned
with proving themselves right (and you
wrong) than they are with understanding
your point of view and coming to a mutually
satisfying agreement.

5. Comfortable with commitment and
intimacy

Secure partners don't mind the closeness
created by a long-term relationship. They
don't worry that you're cutting down on
their freedom or trying to trap them (as an
avoidant partner might) or that you might
find them inadequate or reject them (as an
anxious partner may).

6. Effectively communicates

Partners with a secure relationship style share their feelings and opinion in a clear and straightforward way. They don't expect you to guess what they are feeling or create a scene to get your attention. They are also clear about where the relationship is headed.

7. Flexible and open to adjustment

Secure partners are not looking for a certain kind of partner or relationship. They have a few basic requirements but they are open to various people and arrangements. In addition, they are not threatened by criticism and are willing to reconsider their actions.

The secure partner is not perfect — they have their flaws like everyone does. But a secure partner not only helps to create a healthy relationship but works to keep it that way for the long term.

On the other hand, the "Avoidant' relationship style type has built-in challenges when it comes to relationships.

Avoidant is one of the three main relationship attachment styles. Avoidants are people who wish to keep their distance and minimize closeness in romantic relationships. They are the least happy in relationships, and tend to blame their unhappiness on their partners.

Avoidants tend not to date other avoidants. Two people with this attachment style lack the "togetherness" that a relationship requires.

In addition, avoidants end relationships more quickly. So you are likely to have dated an avoidant in the past or may be now involved with one.

If you are not sure or need confirmation that you are dealing with a person who has an avoidant attachment style, here are the top ten signs your partner is avoidant (in increasing order of importance:)

1. Stresses boundaries

To make sure that their space is not being invaded, avoidants create strict boundaries between themselves and their partners. These boundaries may be physical or emotional sleeping in a separate room or home or keeping insignificant (or important) information from their partner.

2. Uncomfortable sharing deep feelings

Avoidants don't like to share their deepest feelings with their partners; withholding feelings allows them to keep their emotional distance and remain self-reliant. Sharing would bring them closer to their partner — exactly what they want to avoid.

Don't confuse this sign with the anxious partner's apprehension. It's integral to understand why the person is withholding feelings. The anxious person keeps feelings because they fear their partner will not feel the same way as them, or their partner will feel stifled and distance themselves. For the avoidant it's done to keep distance via an emotional boundary.

3. Prefers casual sex

Some avoidants use casual sex as a way to avoid intimacy. They prefer casual sex to sex with an intimate partner because their physical needs are fulfilled but they don't have to worry about caring for their partner's feelings afterward or during. They can also avoid the greater intimacy that results from physical contact.

4. Disregards your feelings

Avoidants believe people are solely responsible for their own well-being and happiness. In relationships they tend to treat their romantic partner like a business partner — they ignore their feelings and respond only to the facts. When confronted they make their partner out to be "sensitive", "overreacting", or "needy".

5. Misses you when apart, but when together wants to escape

Avoidants still have the basic need for love and attachment. So avoidants will miss their partner when they are not around. But if their partner returns, so does the avoidant's feelings of being "trapped", and they feel like they need more space once again.

6. Pulls away when intimacy nears

At the beginning of dating an avoidant you may think everything is going well. They are attentive, loving, and supportive. But as time goes on they find reasons to pull away. They may say things like "the timing is not right" or comment that things are not what they thought they would be.

7. Idealizes a past relationship or partner, or dreams of "the one"

Don't be confused – dreaming of the ideal partner or dwelling on a past relationship does not mean the avoidant wants true love and intimacy; it is an avoidant mechanism. By idealizing a past relationship, the avoidant safely assures they don't have to deal their current relationship.

They convince themselves they missed out on love with some "perfect" ex or that their current partner is not right for them. This way true love and intimacy are always just out of reach.

The two relationship attachment styles detailed are only part the theory results. There is also the "Anxious" relationship style and a combo of the styles for further clarity of why some people can't seem to connect.

Just imagine if you keep meeting this same type of 'Avoidant" personality type over-and-over again? Or are you this type of person? Is it any wonder why your relationships don't work, or last, or seem happy?

Knowing yourself, and your own strengths and weaknesses, is the first step on the road to self-growth and taking accountability for finding, true love, happiness, and maintaining a healthy, functional relationship.

Soulmates and Love at first sight - Fact not fiction

It is said that "love is our search for our alter ego, that part of us that will make us whole again." The great philosopher Plato held the view that, when our souls descended from heaven to earth, they were divided, so when meeting your soulmate for "the first time" in this lifetime, is a sort of reunion.

Should one dare to dream of such a remarkable and mystical encounter? Granted the religious overtone may be a bit disconcerting to some.

The consideration of "love at first sight' is quite literal, but the reference encompasses a myriad of considerations. Love at first, "encounter" may be more accurate, one date, first meeting, or one extended conversation. So what are the precursors of falling head-over-heels in love with someone who you just met? The senses play a role in the psychological aspect of the process.

Cognitive, referring to what he or she says to you that strikes an accord and mirrors your beliefs or disposition. Auditory, simply put, is the appeal of the sound of his or her voice, and if it's pleasing or sexy to you personally, versus in general. Kinesthetic refers to body movement, whether it is graceful, sexy or relaxed. The way she crosses her legs, tosses her hair, or her presence when she enters the room. Or perhaps it's the way he tilts his head towards you when he is listening to you speak, or the masculine way he sits, stands of walks.

Olfactory, in this context refers to how he or she smells, natural, fresh, and fragrance free! Of course fragrance can enhance or detract from the sensation. Tactile refers to the sense of touch. How you feel when you touch his or her hand, or cheek. Perhaps the warmth and comfort of a hug or embrace in greeting or departing. Gustatory refers to the sense of taste, in this case linked to the oral sensation and taste of a sweet Goodnight or goodbye kiss. Naturally, physical or sexual attraction will play a role, the question is whether it's initial, or develops in the scheme of the first encounter. In this day and age can such a wildly romantic notion of instant love have a basis?

According to a survey, fifty-six percent of Americans believe in love at first sight, and the percentage is even higher for married people and those in relationships. This according to CBS dot com, which conducted the 60 Minutes/Vanity Fair poll, surveying 1,100 adults about love, marriage and relationships.

While the Vanity Fair poll may appear anecdotal, a scientific study conducted by the Journal of Neuroscience, proclaims that you can love at first sight and it is connected to a specific region of the brain which is responsible for instant attraction. Now you know, if you meet someone and have an uncanny connection and a visceral gut feeling that he or she is "the one" you may be right.

Part Nine: Out Of the Box Dating Dilemmas

Tired of being single? Buy a mate

Equality of the sexes has been the battle cry of feminist for decades. Equal pay for equal work is the cornerstone of the movement. The equal pay act of 1963 prohibits sex-based wage discrimination between men and women in the same establishment who perform jobs that require substantially equal skill, effort and responsibility under similar working conditions.

According to the National Committee on Pay Equality, the wage gap remained statistically unchanged in the last year. Women's earnings were 77.0 percent of men's in 2011, compared to 77.4 percent in 2010, according to Census statistics released September 12, 2012 based on the median earnings of all full-time, year-round workers.

Men's earning in 2011 was $48,202 and women's were $37,118, a difference of $11,084. In 2011, the earnings of African American women were $33,501, 69.5 percent of all men's earnings, a slight increase from 67.7 percent in 2010, and Latinas' earnings were $29,020, 60.2 percent of all men's earnings, up from 58.7 percent in 2010. Asian American women's earnings at $40,882 dropped from 86.6 percent of all men's earnings in 2010 to 84.8 percent in 2011.

Women are not quite there yet, but the gap is less than it had been historically. Women on average, earn more money now than at any point surveyed dating back to 1960, according to Salary.com. Women are far less likely than men to negotiate at work, which typically costs women more than half a million dollars in earnings over the course of their respective careers, according to Linda Babcock and Sara Lashever, authors of the book "Women Don't Ask."

The authors conducted multiple studies that found that women miss out by failing to negotiate salary, promotions and other advancement opportunities that men commonly and aggressively pursue. On the other hand, women who have business savvy, who've mastered the art negotiation and are more determined to receive their fair share in wages; not only receive equal pay, but higher pay than men in some cases.

Women have fought long and hard to break through double standards on many levels, but there's one double standard that has women on opposite sides of the fence. Women who pay and financially support men.

When a woman stays at home not engaging in paid employment, while her husband works full-time to provide financial support, it seems quite normal. However, when a woman works full-time providing financial support, while her husband stays at home, (without children) seems quite foolish.

According to a survey conducted by Dating site "It's Just Lunch" despite tough economic times and a solid unemployment rate, a new study has revealed that women are "not" interested in dating a man with no job. "It's Just Lunch, surveyed 925 men and women and found that a whopping 75% of women were turned off by unemployment.

The men in the survey were far more open-minded with 46% of those participating in the survey were certain they would date a woman who was out of work, and 19% committing to having 'no reservations' about dating an unemployed woman.

Women who are living this sort of lifestyle, supporting deadbeat husbands or boyfriends, and taking on the role of major breadwinner of the family, creates additional stress which can lead to a number of illnesses.

According to a national survey by Financial Finesse Inc., a California-based nonpartisan organization, women are experiencing much higher levels of anxiety and stress due to financial concerns.

According to the survey, nearly 30 percent of women reported high anxiety levels from financial stress, as compared to 17 percent of men. Furthermore, 9 percent of women responded that they are experiencing 'overwhelming financial stress', as opposed to only 3 percent of men reporting such heightened stress levels. If men are naturally more conditioned to handle finances, perhaps it's best to let a man be a man.

Or at least share financial responsibilities 50/50, it seems fair and much more like common sense. Bottom line ladies, footing the bill for a man and undergoing financial stress, while he lives a kept lifestyle is absolutely absurd.

Buying a man's attention and affection with your money is the act of a desperate woman. And incidentally, having a man indebted to you as his meal ticket is not exactly the romance of the century.

Money won't buy you respect from a man no matter how much you spend. Men aren't wired that way. He'll take your money and treat you like a second class citizen. Instead of receiving the love and admiration you so desperately want, and are willing to pay for, you may end up with a man who is a self-entitled parasite.

You can have true love and still manage to keep your self-respect and dignity in the process. If he truly loves you he will want to take care of you in every way.

A good man will support you in every way, emotionally and financially, and won't leave you holding the bag. Bag of bills, that is. Some traditions are timeless and better to be honored. And so is an old adage with one slight equality update "a fool and 'her' money are soon parted."

Is bad credit a deal breaker for future couple purchases?

High credit scores are a mark of financial stability and offer opportunities to make purchases at a lower interest rate. This could save thousands of dollars in payments associated with major purchases.

Should we request a copy of a credit report from our future spouse before we say "I do?" During the dating process, when getting to know a potential mate, is it okay to ask about their credit history? Overtly sizing up your potential mate's credit worthiness, could leave them a little put-off, right?

Not according to CreditScoreDating dot com, a niche dating site claiming that "Good Credit is Sexy."

Dating couples with uneven credit scores face unique financial problems. The fact is bad credit can affect everything from purchasing a dream home to the cost of auto insurance. A viable option, outside of filing for bankruptcy and waiting it out, is seeking help through a local credit counseling firm

Being diligent about paying bills on time and safeguarding your credit score can prove to be very beneficial in making your dreams come true for a future home purchase.

Dating military personnel and other long-term business transients?

While I'm sure that the personal reasons why someone decides to enlist in the Armed Forces vary from person to person; the decision to remain in the service as a long term career choice, may be no different than pursuing any other long term career niche, in any other work industry.

So what's the difference? Long-term Military VS Civilian workforce careers. Downfalls of military life include various degrees of personal freedom infringements, and the systematic brainwashing that the Military imposes on its lower ranked personnel. You sign-up for the military and they own you. Not a good career move for the independent thinkers.

But, for those who can mindlessly follow orders without reason or rationale, without question, or scrutiny? The military may be a better fit.

In an effort to gain insight as to what drives a person to take on the stripes; here are the top ten reasons for joining the Military, according to U.S. Military Education dot com, which is a military career information and enlistment referral website.

To Serve Your Country – Joining the United States military is often thought of as one of the most patriotic, selfless acts there is. Promoting American ideals of freedom across the world is something many Americans seek to do.

Honor – The military is a storied institution that represents honor at its very core. Many people are attracted to the sense of honor and pride that defending the United States as a member of the military.

Leadership – Military experience teaches valuable leadership skills, skills that stay with you for life. Not only will leadership help you advance in the military, but it will also help you succeed in college and throughout any career you choose after your military service.

To Make a Difference – The military is a wide-reaching organization and positively influences people around the world. Members of the military not only protect the world but also help rebuild and reshape communities.

Benefits – In the Armed Forces, you'll receive an array of excellent benefits. Service men and women and members of their immediate families receive full-service medical, dental and vision care at no cost, as well as an allowance for housing and food. Low-cost life insurance plans are also made available.

Income – The military offers its members a steady, guaranteed salary, plus recruitment and enlistment bonuses and opportunities to advance and make even more money.

Career Training Opportunities – The military trains its members, and trains them well. You'll be trained for your first job, as well as for any positions you might be promoted to. Military training is highly regarded, so the training you receive in the military will transfer to civilian jobs after you' re done serving.

Education – Military members can attend school for little or no cost thanks to the GI Bill, which provides money for tuition, fees, books and other supplies. Educational benefits are available for any college degree level, as well as licensing and certification exams, certificate programs and more.

Travel – Some service personnel have amazing travel opportunities through the Armed Forces and get to see places some people only dream about through different assignments. Traveling the world allows military members to learn about new cultures and meet interesting people.

Job Security – So long as you do your job well and meet expectations, you'll have great job security in the military. The military doesn't't feel the effects of an unstable economy as do most other organizations, so you'll never have to worry about downsizing or layoffs.

Wow! That's quite a bill of goods. The only thing missing in this sales pitch is the Brooklyn Bridge, the kitchen sink, and 40 acres and a mule.

Let's put the conceptual altruism of military service aside for a moment, and examine the reality of committing years of one's life to a romantic relationship with an enlisted career man.

A man who is merely on work assignment in your city, and a relationship that may ultimately go nowhere, as he packs up and moves on to his or her next assignment.

Granted this could occur with any relationship, but the difference here, is you already know in advance that in 2-4 years, he or she is gone.

In some cases there may be a chance that he or she will leave the military. But why waste your time on what might be, when you can have a relationship with a resident, who's here to stay. Choosing a local resident over enlisted military personnel is pretty much a no-brainer. Some military men are looking to play the field and bed down as many women as they can while they are visiting. Others are looking for normalcy and a one-on-one termed relationship, with no promises at the end of his term.

Then there are the ones who make promises that they have no intention of keeping. When their work time is up in your state, they break off the relationship and just leave. Be very wary about any promises or relationships with military personnel or business related visitors. Dating these individuals may not be a good fit for a woman who knows what she wants, a long-term relationship with some semblance of direction, leading to marriage.

Although some of these men may be attractive, extremely fit and charismatic; play at your own risk. I strongly suggest dating locals VS enlisted military men. But if your soldier boy is too irresistible to resist, I suggest you keep it fun, light and platonic and continue to date other men until you find the one who best suits you.

Keep things in perspective; the bottom line is, he's here for a work assignment and moving on to the next assignment after this one is complete.

The alternative is you get married and travel with him? But first ask yourself; are you really military wife material? Living a rootless existence of travel to sometimes less than glamorous locations, deployment separations which can destroy a relationship, brutal combat fears and uncertainties of death, also possible mental health issues such as Post-Traumatic Stress Disorder (PTSD.) It can be a tough call, so choose wisely.

Research References

Plenty of Fish
eHarmony
Match.
Meetup dot com
Sears dot com
Forbes dot com
RedStateDate dot com
BlueStateDate dot com
Health and Human Service Journal of
Family Psychology
DirvorceRate dot com
Forest Institute of Psychology
The Enrichment Journal
Mary Claire Morr-Serewicz, Dept. Of
Human Communications, University of
Denver
Paul Mongeau, Arizona State University
HerWay dot com
"Blink: The Power of Thinking without
Thinking" by Malcom Gladwell
FitnessSinges dot com
FitnessDateClub dot com
Bowling Green State University-Kentucky
Attachment Theory- John Bowlby and Mary
Ainsworth
CBS dot com
60 Minutes dot com
Vanity Fair dot com
Journal of Neuroscience

National Committee Pay Equality

Salary dot com

Linda Babcock and Sara Lashever- "Women Don't Ask"

U.S. Military Education dot com

It's Just Lunch

Financial Finesse

CreditScoreDating dot com

Zoosk dot com